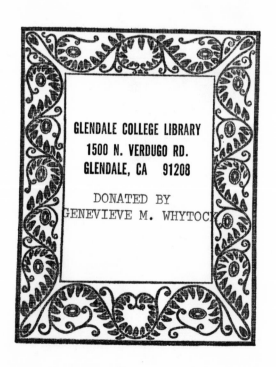

The Handicapped Speak

William Roth

McFarland 1981
Jefferson, N.C., & London

Coauthored by William Roth

The Unexpected Minority:
Handicapped Children in America,
by John Gliedman and William Roth
for the Carnegie Council on Children (1980)

Library of Congress Cataloging in Publication Data

Roth, William, 1942-
The handicapped speak.

1. Handicapped—United States—Interviews.
I. Title.
HV1553.R67   362.4'092'6   80-20297
ISBN 0-89950-022-6

Copyright © 1981 by William Roth
Manufactured in the United States of America

McFarland & Company, Inc., Publishers
Box 611, Jefferson, N.C. 28640

Photographs on pages 22, 126 and 163 are by Jean Gillespie;
those on pages 52, 72, 88 and 98 are by David McGann.

Table of Contents

Acknowledgments   vi

Introduction   vii

Lew Stark   1

Kate Hoffman   20

Don Berry   36

Nancy Kaye   49

Liza DiMaggio   70

Two Children:
  Thomas Brewster   84
  Carl Hershey   90

Maria Sanchez   97

Debra Hamilton   106

Brenda Clark   124

Peter Leech   135

Doe West   159

Don Galloway   181

A Policy Epilog   193
  Transportation   193
  Work   195

Acknowledgments

I have deep thanks.

This book emerged over a period of several years. It was started while I was a staff member of the Carnegie Council on Children. There I would like to thank John Gliedman and Richard Delone. My deepest thanks are to Kenneth Keniston who among other lessons taught me most of what I know about the art and science of interviewing.

For the Institute for Research on Poverty at the University of Wisconsin I have much gratitude. Irwin Garfinkle has been a source of encouragement and sustenance. Felicity Skidmore, Judith Kirkwood and Jan Blakeslee have done noble editorial work.

It was at the State University of New York at Albany that this book was completed. There, the School of Social Welfare gave freely of my time and their support.

Without these institutional affiliations and without these people this book could have been neither begun nor completed.

I also have a great deal of thanks to give to the many secretaries who have transcribed the interviews, including Arlene Gurland, Margaret Jackiewicz, Nancy Wittaker, Ellen Cospito among numerous others.

Robert Franklin, my editor, has been deft and supportive.

Most of all, I wish to thank the people who speak in this book. They have been generous of their time and their patience. Most appear correctly named; a few, for reasons of privacy, have asked to appear pseudonymously. My debt to them exceeds my ability to express it. I hope my thanks may show in small part by the provision of this forum for their important words.

vi

Introduction

A woman in a wheelchair who was qualified for a teaching job was refused it, fought back, and won. Elsewhere, a governor signed a bill prohibiting job discrimination for disabled people. One airline refused to carry a handicapped person; he fought back and won. Another airline published a booklet on special services for disabled people.

Handicapped people in Washington fought to force the inclusion of elevators in the then projected Metro subway system and lost. In another large city, special seats for elderly and handicapped people were marked out on public transportation. A disabled lawyer could not appear at a legal process against him because there was no way for his wheelchair to enter the building; he fought back. A state senate approved bills designed to facilitate access to public buildings and other facilities by disabled people.

The Justice Department charged the world's largest wheelchair manufacturer with collusion, monopolistic practices, price rigging, inordinately high salaries for executives and nepotism. This wheelchair giant has finally come out with an outdoor electric wheelchair, honoring a need met in the breach by small manufacturers, such as an outraged paraplegic who designed a particularly impressive wheelchair, which he christened *Advance,* in a garage.

A computer was developed which transduces printed material into spoken word, a promising use of "space-age technology" for handicapped people. Private groups promote travel by disabled people, package tours, sell sights, and in general open up roads to enjoyment that the rest of us have long expected. The federal government published a book of information for disabled people wanting to use the national park system.

There was a sit-in at the then Department of Health, Education and Welfare regional offices, its Washington headquarters, and the home of the Cabinet secretary demanding that the department issue the regulations for Section 504 of a Rehabilitation Act, which is a civil rights law for disabled people, passed in 1973 and appropriately administered by the Office of Civil Rights. The regulations were issued.

Many disabled people met each other in an atmosphere of friendship and politics at the White House Conference on Handicapped Individuals in 1977. A mayor of a metropolis estimated to have some one million disabled people established an office of the handicapped to amplify the voices of its handicapped citizens. Following hard upon a series of court cases, the Congress of the United States passed in 1975 the Education for All Handicapped Children's Act, providing that handicapped children have the same right to an education as others.

A high school freshman without an arm contested, with the support of his parents and lawyers, a decision excluding him from football training. A person in a wheelchair was kept from a marathon; with American Civil Liberties Union lawyers, he brought the case to the courts and won. A disabled boy scout was denied his eagle badge because of the age he attained working toward it; he fought back and got his badge, making eight other similarly handicapped scouts eligible.

These changes show handicapped people's responses to problems of access, organization, politics, and civil rights, and at the same time, tell much about the way society labels and brands handicapped people. Although there is clearly a physical difference between the disabled and the able-bodied, this is not a decisive denominator of the two groups: what it means to others and to oneself to be handicapped is overwhelmingly social.

It seems hard for society to accept human differences without somehow ranking them, thinking some people to be deficient, dysfunctional. We seem to find it difficult to distinguish between difference and inequality. People are accepted as equal only insofar as they are like most of us. It is to be lamented if blacks must act like whites in order to achieve equality, if women must emulate men, and if handicapped people must aspire to able-bodied behavior and values. For to expect sameness is not only unjust to the minority group from which it is expected, but to a society which has much to learn from the diversity that the members of the group articulate.

The central objective of this book is to make visible the situation of handicapped people and to articulate their views. In fact, handicapped people are already talking to us, not only through words, but through gestures, legislation, litigation, political presence, and other modes of social communication. Having started to think of themselves as a politically disenfranchised and socially constructed minority, the handicapped, as other minority groups, are using the knowledge of their stigmatized identity to change themselves and the society in which they exist. To help change society, to rewrite the social contract, is to emancipate oneself.

As the people who speak out in this book make clear, fundamental changes in public policy are necessary. It is vital that policy makers listen and understand before wasting dollars on ineffective policy. For instance, what kinds of housing, transportation and education are appropriate for handicapped people? The issue of work is of central importance. If many disabled people can and want to work, then the current transfer system which frequently makes work financially costly, must be recalibrated. The current policy, attempting to increase the supply of disabled workers, should be coupled with a policy to increase the economy's demand for disabled workers.

A rethinking is in order; the reasons, escalating costs of the Social Security Disability Insurance and other transfer payments programs, the recent wave of legislation to guarantee rights to handicapped people that the majority of able-bodied American society has taken for granted at least since the Declaration of Independence, the discussion of costs and benefits occurring among policy makers and social scientists, and an emerging political organization of handicapped people which has learned many of the lessons of other minority groups and has begun to impress the needs and requirements of handicapped people on the public and on policy makers.

The "Handicapped" Speak

It is one of the paradoxes of the current situation that handicapped or disabled people have to band together under terms that were originally a mark of social degradation. As yet, the words "black" and "woman" do not have their analog in the language of disability. The issue is still to be decided in the social and political realm from which authentic names are derived. I use the words "handicapped" or "disabled" interchangeably, but ask the reader to recognize that I have done so with knowledge and trepidation. I am aware that the appropriate term has not been agreed upon and that there is some dispute among those who look for a name to make their own. The intent of this book is a learning, an active listening, a recognition of handicapped people themselves. A social science of handicap, or public policy of disability, or a reconstituted social construction of handicap must begin with the handicapped person's assessment of his or her situation. The interviews in this book form a real-world basis from which to launch an interdisciplinary study of handicap, appropriate public policy, and that looked-for social reconstitution.

In what sense are the people who speak in these pages representative of other disabled people? They are not a random sample and as existing statistical efforts are laden with precisely those social views requiring reconstitution, their questions predetermined by the prejudices of the able-bodied world, the people speaking here do not represent a scientific survey.

Who can claim to speak for handicapped people? Surely those who have experienced the immediacy of a handicap. The people who speak from these pages are all incontestable experts in that they have thought long and hard about their problems. They may well sound atypically perceptive and eloquent, for they speak with authority of the problem, situations, and lives of others with handicaps. They are representative, then, in the more traditional political meaning of the word. That is, they speak for others.

The experiential world of disabled people is partially different from that of able-bodied people. In learning something about the experiences of disabled people, which is what these interviews are about, we get clues as to where to start building a new social contract. One of the most prevalent theoretical and experiential frameworks through which handicapped people are viewed comes quite naturally by accepting the standards of able-bodied society, which makes it an easy move to the theoretical standpoint of requiring the adjustment of a disabled person to an able-bodied society. However, for the handicapped person, adjustment in a thoroughgoing sense may be impossible or debilitating; successful adjustment might be a loss for able-bodied society. The premise of adjustment is flawed in the first instance by not knowing which questions are important, or even which issues are questionable. The niceties of curb cuts (for wheelchairs), of not turning right on red (for blind people, and for that matter other pedestrians), and of doorknobs (for people with little hand control) may not arise in the construction of the able-bodied world. Issues in social science such as the psychological development of the handicapped, or even how many handicapped people are unemployed, are hard to question without having some sort of prescientific comprehension of what "handicap" means or the knowledge that a handicap and work are not mutually exclusive.

Having some sort of feeling from within, some sort of story, makes it possible to ask the right questions, to fashion a more just policy, to arrange for a better social contract. That seems to me ample justification for a collection of interviews with handicapped people. Sometimes these interviews suggest answers; always they ask questions; and frequently they provide a starting point for answering the questions.

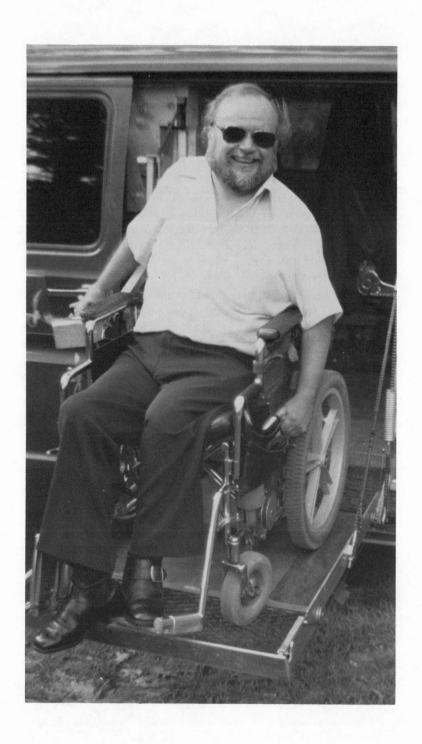

Lew Stark

The places where some handicapped people live may at first blush seem strange. The choice of domicile may be restricted by the absence of wealth if not by poverty. It may be hard to find apartments that accommodate wheelchairs, for example. In one's apartment, it is reasonable to expect more perfect accommodation for any sort of handicap than is mandated by Section 504 in public accommodations. After all, a home should be comfortable.

Sometimes, disabled people live in strange locations. If a person can't drive, he or she may live close to their job or to public transportation. If stairs are a problem, the person will live in a building where they are not needed. Lew drives his own van and uses an electric wheelchair: thus is able to live in a new and cheaply constructed apartment building with an elevator on the very outskirts of town.

It was Sunday when I talked with him and the weekly sailboat races were visible from the terrace. I had known Lew professionally, had known that he could be ornery, but sensed something else. His story is about that something.

"I love to be outside, I love to see things, I love to be with people, I love to participate, and I like to have the feeling that I'm a contributor. Those are my values." Lew's values are those of human beings in a human society. They are so self-evidently human that they often go unstated. But frequently the disabled person cannot take them for granted. This may make that person a connoisseur, appreciative of what is human.

Lew mentions the value of the feeling that one is a contributor. Lew at least is not content with only the gifts of human society; he wants to give to it as well. And he says as much about other disabled people. To deprive disabled people of their ability to contribute, even were it not to deprive them of other goods and services, is to deprive them of part of their humanity. It is a deprivation which should be looked at carefully before being exacted. Perhaps disabled people have nothing, or little, to contribute. But is that true of Lew? And of the other people who speak from these pages? To assume it self-evidently true is an arbitrary injustice toward handicapped people.

The United States, being "affluent," is, more to the point, diverse and complex with many sorts of jobs to be done. There is certainly work for people with variously different bodies. Matching the job to the person may be a difficult matter. The superlative mechanism of the marketplace works roughly here, it needs smoothing. It needs removal of the friction that is discrimination. And perhaps it needs recalibration as well. It is hard to talk to Lew without getting the impression that although he is an abysmal typist, he may have those abilities which we expect in corporate executives. If indeed he does have those abilities, then why is he not a corporate executive? If he has them, he is under-employed and not only he but society is the worst for that. Has Lew achieved the measure of success he has despite a training for failure? Has his handicap excluded him from those social opportunities which are sometimes called "luck?" Is it that the job ladder appropriate to an able-bodied person who would be a corporate executive is inappropriate for Lew? Are there outright forms of discrimination? These are some of the questions society should start asking, not only to be just toward people like Lew, but to be more efficient and more true to itself.

I'm an adult male with rheumatoid arthritis. The main thing about me is, I guess, that I'm in a wheel chair. It happened for the most part in a very short period of time. I think possibly between age sixteen and nineteen it was the worst, and then it left me just about like I am now, except that I couldn't do anything for myself. I had to learn how to do that. It was painful, it was limiting, it was debilitating. It just wiped me out, that's what it did.

I was a heavy little kid—no, actually, I wasn't heavy until I got to be about thirteen or fourteen. So I was a little kid, rode bicycles, played baseball—never very well—did the usual kids' things like swipe vegetables out of people's gardens, played tag, did about average in school—never was much of a disciplinary problem. I had a pretty nice childhood, lived in a lower-class neighborhood I guess it would be called now. I didn't think of it as lower class then because it was my neighborhood, it was just the neighborhood. Also, everybody was a laborer or worked for the railroad or was on the county receiving welfare. The only time I ever thought about growing up was when I was in junior high school and high school, and I expect my role models were teachers and I wanted to become a teacher. However, my family's history is such that practically everybody worked for the railroad, so I probably would have ended up working for the railroad just because it would have been the easiest way.

I had been very sick when I was a child, but I didn't remember that at all. So when I began to get sick I was confused. I kept on doing everything I was doing but on a gradually diminishing basis until I could do nothing. My parents were Christian Scientists and so they weren't overly happy about going to doctors. But I did go to a doctor and he advised at one point that I lie down until the major part of the disease was passed, or the disability or whatever it was. So I did, and when it was I couldn't get up. Now that I look back on it I am sure that he didn't say lie down entirely, but when the disease was at its worst, to try to be resting so I wouldn't hurt myself. But if it went in cycles, during some phases it would have been better if I would have been active. However, I didn't hear that—all I heard was lie down.

How do you feel about the relationship between Christian Science and medicine?

That's a very difficult question for me. I don't know. I think a lot of people delay going to doctors or do not go to doctors because of their religious beliefs—Christian Scientist, or whatever—and they suffer because of it. Well, I guess that's their right, if they want to do that. If they do it to their children I have other questions about it, like can someone really decide for someone else? And I expect they can; when a child is small, they can decide. It's unfortunate, but it does happen. And, I'm sure that a lot of times people receive spiritual benefit from it, but I don't know about that.

I think it's a substitute for medicine. The reason my family was Christian Scientist is that when I had rheumatic fever, when I was small, Christian Science healed me. So they had extreme faith that it was going to do it again. They were Methodist before but they converted.

However, there wasn't really anything available back when I got arthritis that would have made that much of a difference. I could have lived on aspirin and probably had shots and all that stuff, which is still the major treatment of arthritis. There were no hormones. ACTH hadn't been invented. So, possibly the only difference it made in my life is I might now be dead from the different drugs that I had to take, or I would be in the same position I an now.

Were you put in a hospital?

I was never a patient when I was an adolescent. I was totally free of hospitals from age three or four until age twenty, twenty-one. But I resented being treated as a patient. I think it's probably the most demeaning thing that there is. It's being treated as though you were totally incompetent to make any decisions or understand anything that is going on about yourself. It seems to me that medicine treats people very much as if they were all young children. Maybe that's a comfortable category for people to put me in, as though I'm incompetent. But I'm sure that sometimes I use it, you know—if I'm that incompetent well then I'm not responsible and I don't have to do a lot of stuff that other people have to do. I remember I used to work as a social worker in a nursing home and whenever I got really fed up with people coming in with their problems, I would revert to my patient status and sit outside the door with a sort of blank expression on my face and people would never suspect that I was a social worker. They'd assume no one was there and go away.

I spent twenty years in bed. From the age of seventeen and a half maybe, until about thirty-five, thirty-six. At first it was hell. I would wake up at about noon and my mother would bring me something to eat: I would eat in bed, I would wash up and brush my teeth in bed, defecate in bed. My mother would change my sheets while I was in bed. About one or two o'clock in the afternoon I would begin reading and I would read, oh, maybe six or seven hours, and the television would come on and I would watch television until it went off. Then I would read until about five o'clock in the morning, then go to sleep and wake up again around noon. Much of my time was reading, talking to my mother or father or whoever was there. Mostly I was alone. I had one window in my room which I couldn't see out of because it was behind me. I could roll over on my side and see our neighbors. I think there was some sort of a mock orange bush in the summertime and in the wintertime I couldn't see anything. I can still remember the cracks in the ceiling. I can remember all the things that I looked at in the room; that room is burned into my memory forever. I know every inch of it, every inch, floor and ceiling. So, that is what I did.

It wasn't a bad period. I don't look upon it as an unproductive period or even as a punishment period, I look upon it as an unfortunate time. But, rationally, I accomplished a lot of things during that time. I think my reading became so diverse that practically anything anybody gave me I would read. I never bought any books, I borrowed books from everybody. And they would be anything from romantic novels to westerns to philosophy to books on words to some science books. Anything anybody would give me I would read. I subscribed to about four or five magazines and read them every month. So I was, in fact, widening my horizons even while I was in bed, although I didn't realize it. I thought I was just passing time.

I can imagine somebody who is in bed for twenty years just twiddling their thumbs.

I tried that, I tried that. The first couple of years, I had this idea that, first of all, I wouldn't live very long. Well, I hoped I wouldn't live very long. I figured if I lived more than ten years, I would be unusual. So the first couple of years I didn't do anything because my disease was more virulent then, having more of an effect on me and I figured, well soon I'll die. But I didn't, and those were really bad years. Those were years of trauma, and shock, and frustration, and tears and recriminations, and anger, and hatred, and all sorts of things directed at practically anybody who came into contact with me. So I was a bastard then, and I'm still pretty much of a bastard, but not so vocal anymore.

Maybe my family had an influence. They kept bringing me books to read. If they had totally refused I would have probably twiddled my thumbs because there wasn't anything else I could do except what they wanted. I was a prisoner, you know, more or less. I couldn't get out ever.

I come from a family of five. When I first got sick there was mother, father, sister, brother, and another brother. I think my older brother had married and moved out, but I'm not sure. At one point he moved back in because he got a divorce. So, the family was intact in 1946 when I first got sick. By 1952, it was mother, father, brother, and sister. Then my father died in 1952, and it was mother, brother and sister, and then my brother got married — so it was diminishing all the time. And my sister finally got married in fifty-seven or fifty-eight when my mother died.

I was not especially close to my parents. My family was an old German family. My mother and father were both first generation Americans; and grandfathers and grandmothers on both sides came from Germany during the 1870s. My parents were not openly affectionate although I never felt that I was missing anything or unloved either. I always knew that they were there and that they would be there if I needed them, and they always were, and I always knew that whatever happened I would have at least two people on my side. So family was a strong unit and family pride was a strong thing, but as for love and closeness, I don't think so — other than family love, that they belong to you and you belong to them and you are a unit. I think whether I was in a hospital or nursing home or not my family would still be proud of me.

How did your brothers and sisters feel about your disability?

They patronized me. They still do. Well, my sister's dead now, but she always wanted me to do something. She would always bring things home for me to do — jewelry, leather work. I used to paint by numbers, and do all sorts of artsy craftsy things. I used to take courses from DVR by mail, like mechanical drawings, never finished them but I always did well. My oldest brother thought I was a fool to go on to school — I should strike that, foolish, not a fool — that I was just setting myself up to be hurt. He didn't see that there was ever going to be much that I could do and thought that even though I would be broadening my experiences, broadening my horizons, broadening my tastes, when push comes to shove there wouldn't be a job for me and I would spend the rest of my life in a nursing home or something of that sort. He thought that my having learned a lot about life, a lot about the world, and then being unable to experience it was going to be totally frustrating for me. I think he was trying to protect me, I don't think he was trying to deprive me of anything, just to protect me from failure and further frustration.

People try to protect the handicapped that way. I do it myself in my work sometimes. I see people who I think are not going to be employable and then, it's very difficult for me to have them embark upon a career training program just because it's available—when there's not going to be any visible end to it. People cannot keep on going to school for the rest of their lives. Sooner or later they graduate and then there doesn't seem to be very much for them. I've seen people who are almost totally without communication skills go on to school, and through a lot of technical expertise, participate in the school situation. And they should—they're bright and they learn. But when it comes time to graduate and get a job, nobody wants to hire them. So I guess I would like to protect them from having that disappointment, although I work with them and try to develop as much as I can with them. Generally I don't really try to protect them. These are my own philosophical meanderings. I still try to get everybody out there doing what they can; so I guess at that point I have a conflict, but I always resolve it in the client's favor if I can. Even though they might not be employed, that's a problem you have to deal with four or five years down the road.

What was it in your past that made you not give up?

Well, to give up you have to at one point realize that there is nothing you can do. I never got to a point in my life or a point in time like, This is all I can endure—I give up. No matter where I was, if I was in bed, if I was in a hospital, if I was in a nursing home, I still would have been doing something. I have never gotten to the point of giving up. But when I think about the things that I did give up on, they were things that I could realize were not for me. My brothers were good musicians, I was a crummy musician—I gave up on that. I realized that I was never going to be a very good musician. My brothers were athletic, I wasn't athletic—I gave up on that. I realized I was never going to be very athletic or a world beater with my body. But thinking, being, feeling and understanding are participating. I have never gotten to the point where I realized that I couldn't do that, so I guess I just kept on doing it.

I don't know why. I suppose it was because of the way I was raised. My family always expected me to participate at some level and they could just never close the door on me and say, "Well, we give up on you. Forget it. You've just going to be there." I'm sure that they never thought that I would get to be where I am, you know, but it didn't make any difference to them. They would never give up on me, as if I would be nothing, or a thumb twiddler. They always included me in discussions; they asked my opinion on things. They even put me in an elder statesman category where, because I wasn't participating in the front lines, I was therefore more able to think about what was going on and consequently they would listen to something that I said. They made me participate that way, so I guess I never came to the point of *give up* cause I always felt worthwhile

What happened when your parents died?

When my father died it was traumatic—very traumatic, because I really hadn't ever thought about him dying. I figured he would live forever because he had always been there. And I was angered. First of all, my life would have to change, and I didn't like that. Secondly, I was angered because he never really had any chance to enjoy his life. He worked for fifty years for a railroad and a month after he retired he died, so he really never got to enjoy anything. I really don't know if he would have known how to enjoy it anyway—now looking back at it—but at that time I thought it was rotten thing to happen to him. Here he gets to the point of retirement and he's dead, and that really made me bitter. I don't know at who, but just bitter.

I guess I didn't miss him as much as I missed my mother later on because she was the most important person in my life. She was the one that took care of me most of the time. My father helped me and lifted me when I had to be lifted, but my mother did the taking care of. So when my mother died I blocked the whole experience from my mind. I can't remembers what year she died in, although I think it was fifty-six or fifty-seven. I'm pretty sure it was one of those years. That really was a killer. That smashed the family to pieces. The family all went in different directions. My sister and I went in one direction, my brothers went in another direction—just totally demolished the family unit. I keep on thinking of the Bible—when you strike the shepherd the sheep scatter—and that's what happened. Everybody went off on their own. Now they're all established as shepherds in their own families. At that time it was very traumatic. It was my mother who had kept everybody together after my father died.

My brothers separated, and they still have very little in common with each other. They don't really have a brother relationship anymore. My sister, of course, now is dead. I'm the one they all relate to. I can talk to any of them. While some of them don't talk to each other, they can still relate to me, so I've become the center of focus in the family I guess. Maybe when and if I ever get married that will change, but right now I guess I'm the extension of my mother and father in that they recognize they are still a family unit because of me.

So, after my mother died, my sister and I went to Florida and Jamaica with her husband and she cared for me very much as my mother had except that she hired people to help too, especially in Jamaica, where help is really inexpensive. But, my sister died in Jamaica and I had to come back to the U.S. because my brother-in-law was off prospecting for gold in Ecuador. Obviously, he was going to marry again and, since he accepted me because I was his wife's brother and had to be taken care of, he didn't feel that affiliation or that need to care for me anymore. And also I don't think I could have accepted it from him. So I came back to America, to my oldest brother, and lived with him for a while. Then it got to the point where he had to move into a larger home and I realized that much of what he was enduring was because I was there. He had a house that was adequate for his needs; then I moved in and he had to get a bigger house, so that was going to cost him money. Also, his wife had to do a lot of the taking care of me, and that wasn't fair to her or him. So I began looking for ways to get out, either on my own or so that I could help him.

The first thing I did was I went to the hospital. This was in

1961. I hadn't been in the hospital since 1952, when I was very sick. So I went to the hospital and they talked to me about operations that were going to make me walk again. Well, at the point in my life that seemed like a miracle. It would have been great if it could have happened. So I underwent a lot of operations, some retraining, some occupational therapy, until I got to the point where I could propel my own wheelchair, get up out of bed by myself, dress myself, feed myself, wipe my butt—you know, all the activities of daily living. That's when I started in school. So, from about 1964 I was in a wheelchair.

My brother moved out into a suburb and it would have been impossible for me to commute everyday to go to school. So I moved into a nursing home and lived there for seven years, while I was going through my undergraduate career. Then I moved into another nursing home where I was employed to develop an independent living floor for disabled young adults and also as an assistant social worker. I lived there for two and a half years. Then I got a job in another nursing home and I worked there for about three months and I was fired.

Why were you fired?

It's a long story. I was fired because the owner said I was incompetent and incapable of doing the job I was hired for. He said it was because of my physical disability, so I filed discrimination charges against him with the Department of Industry, Labor, and Human Relations and I won. It was very traumatic to be considered incompetent in your first job, but the real catalyst that caused the firing was the fact that the administrator who had hired me, who had worked with me the three months that I was there, was leaving. I really feel the employer was somehow trying to strike back at the administrator or damage the administrator's reputation by firing me. I don't think he had any personal bad feelings about me; it was just that he wanted to strike back, and he probably also believed my disability kept me from doing a good job, which it didn't.

When I couldn't find a job after I got fired, I was frightened. Probably the most beautiful summer that God ever created and I couldn't enjoy any of it because I was out on my own living in an apartment by myself, living on unemployment compensation, and I couldn't find a job. All I could think about was finding a job and getting to work, you know, getting something. I read the ads, I applied at job service but DVR didn't help me. I went to job interviews looking for jobs; I was never hired. Finally, I saw an ad in the paper one day, I called up the people, and I got a job. It was medical coordinator for the personnel pools that handle short term or temporary professional help. Medical coordinator is a euphemism — what they really meant was a person who would be on the phones dealing with clients, dealing with staff, trying to coordinate the needs of clients with the abilities and time frames of staff. So, I did that. I worked there for about a year until I finally got a job with the Division of Vocational Rehabilitation, which just about brings us up to date. Part of the time now I work for the Division of Vocational Rehabilitation as a rehabilitation counselor and part of the time I work for the Department of Administration, developing a training manual for affirmative action for the hiring of the handicapped. So, I have two jobs.

These jobs and your current job are all within the context of disability. Why is that?

Well, that is what I was trained to do. I have my master's degree in rehabilitation counseling. It was my decision to work in things connected with disability, in so far as that's where the jobs were. Also, there was money available for that. I didn't think of myself as having unusual skills in other than a behavioral area. I don't think I could have made it as an English major. I was always interested in history and political science but I didn't see that there was going to be that many jobs available in that sector. So, I guess it was a decision based upon, first of all, what was available, and secondly, my perception of that job market. I was interested first in helping myself.

Now I've got to the point where I'm established, I think, where I'm reasonably independent economically, where my needs are taken care of for the most part. Now I can begin to look at things from other than my own point of view. I've always felt, even way back when I was working in a nursing home, that the way disability or disabilities per se were being handled was not right. I've always had the idea that there should be a way for disabled people to participate more fully in their society and their community, that somehow the needs of disabled people, other

than to keep them alive and insulated in a nursing home, had to
be considered, which is why I worked at trying to develop a unit
for physically disabled young adults and why I worked as a coordinator for activities for mentally retarded adults.

How did you get training for your job?

I sometimes think about that. I never really understood how
that happened. I didn't have any great desire to do it. It was
something to do to keep my mind stimulated, something to keep
me occupied. I don't think I was trapped into it, although I
sometimes feel that I was trapped into finally going to work. I
loved the school part. I thought that was the most stimulating,
mind-expanding thing that I had ever been involved in. Much
more than high school or than junior high school or grade
school.

First of all I learned how to be a negative retoucher. I went
to a training program that lasted one week. I started doing that
and I was getting paid ten or fifteen cents a negative, which
meant that I was earning thirty-five to fifty dollars a month,
which wouldn't support me. Then I wanted to go into air brush
rendering, which is a step higher than negative retouching and
pays about twenty dollars an hour. To train for that I had to be
considered a full time student. I had to take other credits, so I
took academic credits at a vocational school and did very well.
But I didn't do so well at air brushing rendering. The distances I
had to cover with the air brush were greater than my range of
motion would allow. So there came a point where I recognized I
could not do air brush rendering, I couldn't make a living as
a negative retoucher and DVR was available to me. So I went on
to school and I went to college and got a bachelor's and a master's.
That's how it happened.

How important is it to you to live independently?

Sometimes it makes me feel good that I am able to live by
myself. Lots of times it's just lonely, but I think it's lonely for a
lot of people, whether they are physically disabled or not. I don't
think about it as value thing, I think about it as something I do,
that I have to do in order to survive and I do it.

My values aren't that I can get up and dress myself and feed
myself and do my laundry and things like that. My values are
more like I love to be outside, I love to see things, I love to be

with people, I love to participate, I love to be stimulated, and I like to have the feeling that I'm a contributor. Those are my values. Like people ask me questions: sometimes I have answers, sometimes I have knowledge, sometimes all I have is just the ability to listen. Those are the things that are valuable to me because I do them well, I guess, and I enjoy doing them. I enjoy being outside, I just enjoy somehow breathing and seeing the sky, you know, I guess it's the sort of foolish ecstatic values that don't have any real importance. I enjoy art and music and things that make me feel good. Those are the things I like.

My own feelings are that if a person can live independently they should live independently. That's another one of my values. I think it's important to live independently because that is how you have the most opportunity to be and do and see and feel yourself. Anytime that you move somebody into a nursing home or into a protected atmosphere, that independence somehow diminishes. It shouldn't perhaps but it does. So I guess I accept those institutions at their present face value and realize that they exist for a very narrow purpose—to keep people alive, return them to some stable physical or mental condition, provide them with the bare minimum of support necessary to keep them alive. This is not a purpose that is always in line with individual self-actualization.

As I was going through my preparation for whatever jobs that I've had, I could see the problems most disabled people have. First of all they have no transportation mechanism that's going to get them from where they live to a job, which leaves two alternatives: either you prepare people to work independently at home or you get disabled people into groupings where they can establish businesses of their own and don't need transportation. I think people should be expected to or at least have the opportunity to contribute as much as they can in whatever way they can at all levels of disability—whether it's physical or mental. Sometimes it's necessary to provide an alternative other than sheltered work, and the alternative should be or could be something that they could evolve and work into by themselves along with other disabled people as a sort of disabled community. I think that has been accepted and established in Europe where such communes or communities exist. In the Netherlands I know they exist, and I think they exist in Sweden and Denmark. In that way, everyone could contribute. They wouldn't have to travel; they could *be* there. So, I think offering people the opportunity to contribute as much as they can or as much as they want to is an important change in the traditional handling of disabled people.

Now they are not offered the opportunity to contribute; they are provided a maintenance type situation. Their medical needs are met to keep them alive, and they are given a minimum amount of money so that they can at least have the minimum amount of life support systems, like they can get electric wheelchairs if they have to (providing they are not in a nursing home), or they can have money for going out or buying cigarettes, or buying toothpaste and things, through the different programs.

How do you feel about sheltered workshops?

I have lots of feelings about sheltered workshops. Some of the feelings are very good. I know there are exceptional sheltered workshops where the client participates at the utmost level. And I know there is the opposite too, where they are just a dumping ground, where you put the people you don't want to keep in the nursing home or in the developmental disability center. The sheltered workshop could be a very dramatic force in disability, but I don't know how to make it that and, in fact, I haven't really thought about how it could be changed very much. I think the people who are managing sheltered workshops have a tremendous responsibility. Some of them are meeting it well, innovating, expanding, and developing new products and primary manufacturing situations for their people. I think that developing primary manufacturing so you have a viable product, and hiring disabled people to work at it and getting some subsidy to do it might be one of the real evolutionary things that's going to come out of sheltered workshops. I don't know about the make-work things. I don't like those—where the people in one section pack checkers and the people in the next section unpack them. I don't think that's productive but in some cases it may very well be necessary. I think sheltered workshops should be one step, one stage in helping people to become viable economic personalities. And I think pretty much of everything is economics; where the money is, that's where the action is.

As people become independent economically their feelings about themselves change. This is probably another value system and this might be part of the Protestant ethic. But in the future work will have to be looked upon as something other than what it is now. To me, work now is earning a living, paying taxes — part of the Protestant ethic or whatever, very competitive. Society will have to change in the direction of each working according to his ability rather than competing with everybody for what exists. I think society will have to become more flexible to change in that direction. I think society will be different in the future than it is now. I don't know whether better or worse, all I know is different. Better or worse sounds like a value judgment. I would hope that it would be more accepting and if it is accepting it should be more open. I think sheltered workshops can contribute to that. But there has to be another step between sheltered workshops and full competitive employment, and I don't know exactly what that step is.

Do you think laws like 504 are making it more open?

Yes and no. I think laws like 504 help and I think laws like 504 are not the last laws we're going to see like that. I think there is going to be more enforcement before there can be less enforcement. So I expect such laws are acting as catalysts; they are forcing change. And maybe the only way change ever occurs is by force, pressure.

If you had a time machine now and could go back and advise yourself at age eighteen, what would you whisper in your ear?

I'd say invest in the stock market, take your savings and start buying A.T.& T. and Xerox because by now I'd be very wealthy. Other than that, I guess I'd say be more militant and fighting than I was then. Fight for yourself, not for everybody else. Participate more, not just in the family but in the community. Be more militant in standing up for your own values rather than trying to always see the other person's point of view. Try to know yourself enough so you could identify what is primary in your thought system at that time and fight for it.

You were a delegate to the White House Conference on Handicapped Individuals. What do you think you contributed and what do you think you learned?

I think I learned more than I contributed. That was my first experience in a national situation. I was overwhelmed by the number of people with disabilities that were there. All of a sudden I came face to face with them and it brought me to the point where I suddenly realized these numbers exist. These people exist. Their problems exist. There were hundreds of them, thousands perhaps, people in wheelchairs, on crutches, on stretchers, all sorts. That was a tremendously vital situation for me to be in. They were all capable of contributing, and they all contributed to the best of their ability, so that was the thing that I got out of it most. Also, I like to think that all these people together became visible to the country as a whole, even though the press coverage for the most part wasn't very good.

How did I contribute? I think I contributed in my state caucuses, by listening and judging and weighing and evaluating the things that people said, and contributing occasionally myself. I think I contributed by going to meet with our state representatives. I contributed by participating in the workshops. How much that contribution is going to change anything is moot. Perhaps in the long run changes will occur because of it. Whether they occur in line with the recommendations and priorities that we worked on or some synthesis of those priorities and recommendations is another thing, but I'm sure that change is going to occur. I think change is inevitable. I also think I contributed by just being there, enduring the kinds of physical torture involved with just being there. I'm sure that for some people the facilities were worse than they were for me and I'm sure that for some people they were better than they were for me, but for me they were less than ideal. I would have liked to have had the opportunity to participate at a higher level, maybe at the White House level. I don't know how one goes about that though—I think it's possibly political. I'm not very political, but all in all I think I benefited from it and I contributed to it, not necessarily in the same ratio. I think I benefited more than I contributed.

Did the experience change you in any way?

I don't know. I incorporate change so easily into my system that sometimes I am not aware that change has occurred until I look back years later. Yeah, strangely enough I began to see disability from both the point of view of being disabled and the point of view of being able-bodied and I endured some of the delays and the lack of patience that able-bodied people must feel with the disabled. Things didn't come easily for the people that were around me. That made me impatient. I wanted things to go quicker somehow, to be more facile, more productive. How did it change me? I guess it made me more determined and more militant. It made me recognize that the needs that exist are overwhelming, and unless they are met, a tremendously large section or proportion of this population is going to be eliminated from all economic consideration. I cannot see the country forever being able to maintain people who are not productive, who are not contributing, even in a limited way. There has to be some way which people can be maintained other than just for the purpose of maintaining them. I think—I don't know about every handicapped person—but I think a large number of them can be more productive than now. I don't know if everybody can be productive, but I don't think you can afford to have thirty-five million who are unproductive.

Why do you think that's the case now?

I think it's largely a matter of attitudes. I think it's also a matter of economics. The priority systems have been such that they have excluded handicapped people rather than included them. "Handicapped" doesn't exist in a lot of people's consciousness. They see people with handicaps as charity cases, more to be pitied than to contribute. Consequently we've had an attitude of grudgingly providing only the minimums for these people. We haven't really worked at finding ways to include them so that they can contribute. I'm sure that there are all sorts of factors involved. I suppose it's a traditional feeling. There have always been exceptions, but there are exceptional people in any population of individuals. I think of Steinmetz, who did so much for electricity and worked for Thomas Edison and General Electric. He was a dwarf, or a misshapen man, and I'm sure that he was excluded from everything, yet I think he had a wife and a family. But always these people have been on the periphery. Their contributions have been welcomed when available, but they still have not been incorporated into the body politic.

I guess it's because people try to look away from unpleasantness or threatening things. You look away from illness because you don't want to be ill. You look away from ugliness because you don't want to be ugly. Not all handicapped people are pleasing to look at, sure, but I don't think that anybody is totally pleasing to look at. Plato had an idea about what beauty was and I don't know that any of us measure up. But insofar as they are departures from the norm, the more a departure they are the less they are considered acceptably beautiful. We're trained from small on that there is a physical ideal or a mental ideal and that people who don't conform to that ideal are somehow different, to be watched and to be not trusted, and to be approached very cautiously, patronizingly, or not at all. It's unfortunately a white ideal, I think. I think it's part of the problem that the blacks have had, it's part of the problem the minorities have had, it's part of the problem that all people who are different have.

Those who are different have not really been allowed to be in the mainstream. We haven't been able to vote in the public polling place, and women didn't get the right until 1919, you know; some blacks still don't have the right to vote. So I guess lack of participation makes us all similar, and a lack of recognition of whatever we have to contribute. In a sexist world, women are considered sex objects. In a segregated world, if you are not white you're excluded because of your color. In an economic world, if you're not capable of full competition then somehow you're excluded and not considered. And I guess that's how we're similar. We're all anxious to participate, but from prejudice or lack of understanding have not been allowed to, and finally we're forcing the issue. In that way we're similar too — forcing our way into the community.

How do you feel interacting with women?

I think twenty years in bed hurt me a lot. It was socially a big chunk out of my life. I think possibly I'm interacting at a social age that's different from my chronological age. Which is okay. Most of my friends are younger. I don't think that any of them are thirty. It's not comfortable all the time to be with women; it's not comfortable all the time to be with men. I think I would like to have more interaction but I don't necessarily know how to go about it other than the way I am, and that's by reinforcement and trial and risks. I think everyone has to go through that. I'm just going through it a little bit later than other people.

I would very much like to be a stud, but I'm not. I don't have women beating down my door to get at me, which is unfortunate. I would enjoy the attention, but I think I've developed an idea of self worth because of my situation, that I have to be worthy of myself before I can be worthy of somebody else. I don't have the physical attributes, the strength, and smoothness, the suave ability to be overwhelming for women or for other groups. I have to deal with people on the basis of what I'm worth, who I am, and where I'm coming from — and hope that someone else can see those features. And if I show them enough maybe somebody can.

On occasion you've struck me as having a certain amount of anger in you.

I have a lot of anger in me. It's just a question of who it's directed at. Sometimes, or mostly, the anger is directed at myself and that's self-defeating and I'm getting over that. I'm learning how to express anger, and the more I learn the less angry I think I will become. But I haven't learned it all yet. I'm still angry — at society, at the community, at the system. I think anger is part of my motivating force. As long as that anger exists I will be out there in the field, motivating, causing confrontations, acting on confrontations, and striving for what I want, for what I think should be. So I think anger in that sense is good. If I was totally happy I don't know what I would be. Probably nothing.

Kate Hoffman

Kate's is very close to a purely socially constructed handicap. There are few things she cannot do; there is no chronic illness underlying her handicap; she simply does not have one hand.

Apparently the medical system was the main lightning rod for her social attribution and definition. She made many trips to the hospital, never being cured but perhaps returning with thoughts different from those gone with—a new conviction that she was different, that the difference was medical, that she was sick, and that although she could not be cured, she should be cured.

Kate identifies herself as handicapped and her society does the same. Thus it would not be fair to assume that Kate's handicap derives solely from her interactions with the medical system. Yet not to believe that the medical system is central in the social construction of handicap is to ignore the obvious. A person with a handicap is first called sick; when it becomes evident that the handicap will last indefinitely the label changes to handicapped. Yet much of what it means to others to be sick carries over. A person is treated as a patient and if a child, his or her family may also be treated as patients. With Kate the medical system would not accept that it could do nothing. In what her physicians no doubt conceived of as the most enlightened of medical care they did something: they amputated the stubs on her hand; they kept tabs on her; they gave her a hook.

Regarding these circumstances it is easy to conclude that medicine should have paid more attention to the whole person instead of the hand. So doing, the argument might go, it would have been more sensitive to her psychological and sociological situation. In that event it would hardly have subjected her to

20

degrading clinics where there was little or no chance for success;
so doing, it would hardly have given her a hook; so doing, there
is at best much doubt that it would have cut off part of her body
at a young age. Thankfully, medicine is becoming more
enlightened. But such an enlightened psychosocial medicine
miscalculates if it reckons Kate's encounter with a friend, her
family, her body to be in the first instance medical problems. For
these are problems of life like those that in one form or another
we all face. To the degree they are defined as medical, the
"patient" loses responsibility and autonomy in the rest of her life.
To this degree also society will tend to perceive her as a case in-
stead of a person.

It would seem that the first decision medicine must make is
where and when to intervene. Obviously there are reasons to in-
tervene with disabled as with able-bodied people. But to
surround the disabled person with what Michel Foucault has
called "the clinic" is inevitably to deprive him or her of
humanity—permissable and necessary in the case of acute illness,
dangerous when necessary in the case of disability.

Kate's response was exceptional. After some years she
escaped from the clinic. She went through elaborate maneuvers
to pretend to her doctors that she was a good patient with full
command of her hook. And she gradually evolved her identity as
a human being in the face of the clinic. How many handicapped
people do not escape?

One of the obstacles that Kate encountered in her social
recovery had to do with the reclamation of her sexuality. This in-
trinsic right of human beings is frequently not even regarded as a
live question with the disabled. Society closes the door, locks it,
and forgets about the key. The development of sexuality becomes
difficult if not impossible.

For those people disabled from birth or in childhood the
situation is yet more difficult. The answer of a parent to the
disabled child's question about sex may be couched more
carefully than answers to an able-bodied brother or sister. The
disabled child may engage in little body contact wth other
children. From noble motive teachers at school protect the
disabled child from sex. I am reminded of an instance where a
teacher, no doubt out of a desire to protect the child, encouraged

him not to participate in square dancing. A week later the same child made excuses to be absent from an out of school sixth grade party where he knew that spin-the-bottle would be played. That same child the next year went to an all boys' school. Another 18 year old whom I met professed his hatred of women. Casualties these, of a sometimes fight that society has with disabled people. In Kate's case the fight was won but in other cases it is not. Does it have to be a fight?

I am a thirty-two-year-old disabled women. I was born with a congenital disability—a loss of my right hand. There's no real explanation of it. I was a change-of-life baby and people talk about why that should have an impact. I've never heard anything that made sense about that. Really no one knows. There's no history of it in my family and there's been no explanation, which I think has been difficult because it means grappling with the totally unknown. It would have been much easier for me to be angry at times in my life, if I could have had a specific focus for the anger. I think something like an accidental trauma might have facilitated my getting a handle on my feelings sooner. For many, many years I was in various kinds of therapy and never really dealt with what the impact growing up different meant in my personality development. I think part of that was that I just didn't know how to get angry. Who could I be angry at?

I have a sense that I'm dealing with something that was clearly fatalistic. There was a sense of destiny about it that constantly reminds me that I'm not in charge of who I am. That's always been something that's troubled me. As a child one of the thoughts that constantly gnawed at me was, "why me?" There was never an answer to it and I know that. I went to the Shriner's Hospital from age three to sixteen, every six months, and I never understood the reasons for that either. I don't know what the hell they were watching in my development. One of the few things that they concluded was that I was ambidextrous. Anyway, I've always done things left-handed, needless to say, without that much difficulty, so I don't know what that means.

How old were you when you first noticed that your body was different?

I can't focus on one specific memory, but a whole series of memories starts with the Shriner's Hospital experience, when I was three. The hospital experience was awesome! I hated it!

What were they trying to do?

I don't know. Apparently I was born with a couple of extensions where fingers would normally be. They were not enough to be functional. When if was five, they decided to remove them. It was a very small minor operation, but I was child of five and the whole hospital ethos was troubling from the day I walked in. It was terribly inhuman and I was fearful. I think part of this was a sense that I was a totally passive figure in the hands of this cold force around me. Of course it made me angry, even as a child of three, when I would ask, "Why am I coming here?" and I would always get some vague answer like, "Well, we're going to watch your growth and see if we can do anything for you." It's hardly sufficient. It was also frightening because I knew that I was dealing with something different and unknown and the doctors seemed to have some ideas about it but it was clear they weren't going to share them with me. So it capitalized on this almost existential terror that I had of what being different really meant. Where did it come from? What did I do? Am I being punished for something?

Looking at you, I get the picture of somebody whose body is exceedingly stable, who's missing one hand, but otherwise is entirely normal, and I can't really understand why you went to a hospital for thirteen years. Hospitals are to treat diseases, and looking at you, there's nothing they could have done except find the hand and glue it back on.

That's right! Exactly! I also want to say that I was raised Catholic. My parents were not particularly religious, but I was raised in the concept of sin. That was thread that went along with this. I couldn't understand why I was going to the hospital. I felt healthy, normal. I was always considered a fairly bright child, very bubbly and happy. I had a lot of confidence in myself and the Shriner scene seemed out of context to me. It reminded me that there was something radically wrong.

Another very important issue arose for me through the Shriners right from the beginning. This was that I remember my mother sitting and waiting, trying to establish rapport with the other parents who were there. There was always an element of tension; you know, it's not a normal setting. Everyone, I'm sure, had the same discomfort in a setting which represents something negative. But compounded with that was that there was very little opportunity for any formal interaction. There was never a social worker, or any specific channel for patients or parents to deal with any of these things. In those long waits, we children would be standing in our little johnnies and all the mothers would be sitting together chatting. I could pick up their tension and their longing to break out of this setting and to connect elsewhere, because there clearly was a very strong thread that connected these people and it couldn't really develop in a hospital setting. I was impressed with that, repeatedly, every time I went, always wondering if there wasn't something that could be done for my mother.

In recent conversations, my mother and I have had a lot of discussions about what it was like for her in the first couple of years of my life, getting adjusted to being proud of a child who was different. There was a lot of denial that she lived with for most of my life. She talked very freely about the discomfort of taking me in public, you know, even driving me around in a baby carriage when I was very small, how difficult it was for her. I remember times when there were extended family gatherings, and I sensed a little bit of tension.

One other issue at the Shriner's Hospital that was very important for me was that I was around kids who were much more seriously disfigured than I. Many of the people there always said, "Look at you, you're healthy." I mean I was apparently the least affected person in that population. I always saw other children with no arms and no legs, and children with lots of internal problems. I never quite understood what they were, but I knew that some of them were quite serious. And I knew that there was a lot going on around me, a lot of very serious situations where people's lives were more heavily involved than mine. The guilt trip always came up because people laid their concept on me that I was the healthy one there and wasn't I lucky? I never quite knew how to deal with that. What can you say?

Have you ever found out why your mother kept on taking you?

I came from a blue-collar family that didn't really have a rational approach to these sorts of things. Doctors told them that I should go; the doctors dictated what the norms were. They were the type of family, despite the fact that my father was very, very bright and I'm sure was terribly troubled by these same questions, that would never question the doctor's rule. It was the doctor who made the next appointment and the doctor who said "we think it's a good idea for you to come every six months, maybe some new developments will come up, maybe some new devices will come up." My parents weren't ready to challenge that. If a new device came on the scene, there's no reason the doctors couldn't inform me through the mail and I wouldn't have had to come every six months to hear them say there was nothing new. I feel that I was there not only as a research subject but to pacify the doctors. I mean, it seems as though they could not look me in the eye and say "There's nothing I can do for you." They couldn't deal with their own limitations.

Do you have any brothers or sisters?

I have one older sister—four years older. My sister and I have had a very intense rivalry. I've never really been extremely close. We're very different personalities and I think that accounts for a lot of it anyway. I believe that my parents treated us very much equally; I can rarely remember a time when they singled me out, particularly in relation to my disability. In many ways my family was very accepting of me. But it's always been very clear that I would be the career girl. It was a given that I would go to college and have a career. The implicit innuendo was "she won't get married." My sister got married at twenty-two. She had a very difficult time in college and got married the year after finishing. She is now living in middle America with her two kids.

How did you get along with the kids on your block and kids in school?

Fine, I always got along well with kids. I was happy, but compliant. This is important because I had a very strong personality and yet was compliant. I could be a brat at times I'm sure but I never challenged where it counted. When it came to children, I remember it was somewhat difficult meeting a large number of new kids because that always meant having to listen to them making comments about my hand and having to always deal with that. Usually kids started out with, "Gee, that's ugly! What happened to you?" And my rote response was "I was born that way." But what did that mean? It didn't answer anything! It was enough though, to get it out in the open and then children would adapt and adjust and accept. So essentially the only obnoxious thing was getting to know new people and having to go through that interaction.

In fourth grade I was becoming fairly popular in school. I remember I had a couple boyfriends, I had someone's ring. And then I started going through a gawky stage, part of which I atrribute to an experience with the Shriner's Hospital where the doctors *finally* found the answer for me! They *suddenly* realized what they could do to help me. The irony here for me is that it was really clear that this was an answer that had been open to them all along. It was suddenly that, you know, they made the move. I had no choice but to respond. And the move they made was that they were going to give me this hook. You know, the typical iron hook. The day they told me at the Shriner's, when I was ten standing there in my underpants naked from the waist up, they were *so* unbelievably disgusting—professional, distant, condescending! I came home and I cried as if the world had died for me that night. I cried and cried and cried and cried. I saw that hook and it was ugly and repulsive and disgusting! An iron hook! It was the most disgusting thing I could think of. My parents were distraught, too, because they weren't happy with that decision, but their only thought was that we've got to give it a try.

They fitted me with this hook, this heavy thing that took away my sensitivity. They put me in the Shriner's Hospital for two weeks to teach me how to use it, which is utterly absurd. The principle of using this hand, I got in half a minute. It moves by flexing one's shoulders forward, and after you try it a few times, you get a sense and you know that it's the kind of thing that you have to experience and that only time will teach you how much force one needs to put into opening it—the leverage action.

All my worst fantasies or experiences in going each six months to the clinic, of being around kids who were more disabled than I, in a setting that was grotesque, cold, without my family, without any support network, were confirmed. I was enraged about this for years. I once got in touch with this in an analytic session and the only words that could describe it were "green vomit!" My whole system became green vomit when I associated with the Shriner's.

You're not wearing a hook today so obviously at some point you said no.

Well, I said no right from the moment I saw it, I'm sure. What happened was once I got home from the hospital I put the hook away, and only took it out the night before I went to the Shriner's every six months. There was one other interaction. I wore it once to school. All the people who very much accepted me up to that point were repulsed by it, had very strong reactions, and of course, all the kids immediately called me "Captain Hook."

But the doctors never understood my emotional state. They not only didn't understand, but I felt they didn't want to hear it. So we played a game for the next six years, where I would go and they would ask me how it was, and I would say it was fine. And every single time the next question was, "And you wear it all the time?" I'd say yes, and I'd smile and lie. And of course, they knew I didn't wear it all the time. My father would tell me the night before, "You know, you can't go and say that again." This hand was sparkling clean. I would sometimes rub dirt onto the harness and the back to make it look dirty. But, you know, the whole thing looked brand new anyway and I'd see all these kids with their worn prostheses; I knew the difference in appearance. But we'd go through the charade every single time. The doctors kept it up themselves for six years. My chart says "remarkable progress."

The other thing happening about this time was tied in with confirmation, in sixth grade. I was 12 then. The changes of puberty and the humiliation of standing naked before doctors in the clinic setting were traumatic. These feelings compounded the lie about wearing the hook.

I'd go to confession; I always knew that I was lying to these doctors, knowing that they knew the lie, and knowing that the arm cost about a thousand dollars to be made and that's an expensive hand so I should be wearing it. I was equating a thousand dollars with a mortal sin. In the Catholic Church, you may know, there's mortal sin and venial sin. Venial sin can be wiped away with a few Hail Mary's, but with mortal sin you go to hell. I was convinced that mine was a mortal sin and I was going to go to hell because I wasn't using my arm and was lying about it to these doctors who knew.

There was some awesome sense about this whole sin-concept that kept building up. That was something that I lived with for a long time. Long after I gave up any concept of sin, there was still the sense that my disability had a lot to do with my guilt and my lying. Even when I was in analysis dealing with other things, I always knew that I had to deal with why I was afraid I was going to go to hell because of my mortal sins.

How did having a disability affect your social interactions with boys?

I became increasingly less popular till seventh grade when I totally withdrew after the spring dance. I remember it well. Everyone was pairing off and the popular kids date the popular kids. I was an outsider, I was not invited. By that time it was very, very clear that I was totally at the bottom of the social caste. Finally this one boy invited me and he was, you know, a real twirp in the class. From there on, I knew I was on the outs.

What happened is I went underground. I became very sublimated into tasks, and interests, and hobbies and doing well in school. I always got straight A's all throughout school. Having a B was a major calamity. I worked hard at it. I applied myself. And I thought I was happy. I knew that it made me very uncomfortable at some level when other kids started going off to pajama parties and that I was not dating. But I always smiled it away. This is my compliant side. At some level I knew and hated this compliant aspect of myself even then, but I couldn't challenge that.

I never had a place socially in high school either. I was not one of the really bright kids. I was near the top of the class but I was never one of the five or six kids who were really creative. I knew that there's a difference. I knew they were always three steps ahead of me in their analysis of something. I could do well because I could study and I still would memorize stuff. I was certainly not one of the in-people, one of the football crowd. I was visible a lot because I was in a lot of activities and lots of people knew me. I'm sure everyone must have thought I was a sweet girl, you know, that's the kind of image that people have of me. But I was shy. I never really had an identity, just sort of as *outsider*.

I denied the hurt. It had to be my hand; I was imperfect. That was what made me the outsider. I was aware of the gawkiness that I was going through, like wearing glasses. I was dealing with my disability all the time, but I would never tell people that. Peoples always *assumed* I was very well adjusted. No one ever questioned that. But at some level of my being I knew that every moment of the day, every hour of the day, I was dealing with my hand in some way, always compensating. I made that connection but I never explored it. That was always my secret.

Then I went to college and they had these awful mixers. I went to a Catholic girls' college. The reason I went to a Catholic girls' college was, because I wanted to study and get good marks. My father told me you didn't get good marks if you went to a big school and partied, and I didn't need to party because I was going to be a career person. In retrospect, it's obvious that I was terrified that if I went to a place where everyone was mingling I would be out of it again and I couldn't take that anymore. I would have to create a positive identity for myself and the only way I could do it was being away from men because at least I knew I could do well in the school. Anyway I went to this place and was miserable for four years. Miserable!

Part of it was the stilted, artificial contact one had with men through mixers. Guys stood on one side and women stood on the other, and the cool men went over and looked at the beautiful women and picked out the one they wanted. I would sometimes pick up a loser type, you know. I was very uncomfortable. I would *love* to dance, and I really am a fairly coordinated person, but there was the whole big question of, when is he going to see my hand. I was *very* good at hiding it; people lived with me for months and didn't know about my hand — didn't notice!

I have various kinds of concealing habits. I always carry books over my arm and I put my left arm and hand over my right and I always had something in my hand, or skirts with pockets. I could even get away with dancing; I was clever enough and manipulative enough to figure out moves that would just be cool.

Many times I could be with people for several dates and no one would ever notice. But there was always this huge dilemma of "when do I tell him?"

What did people say when they found out?

It ran the range. Usually if people noticed right away, they didn't ask me for another date. The common response was, "Oh, you poor thing. How'd it happen? Can you drive a car?" A few basics like that. You know, in the dating situation they'd never really talk about it—just the guy would say, "ooohhh," and be very polite and cordial, but I knew when someone was sort of turned off. I could tell that everything was going fine and the person was really engaged, and then suddenly was just not there anymore. It would never really be discussed. He'd say "Fine, I'll call you again." And he'd never call.

When did you grow up sexually?

During college, there was a boy, to whom I was very much attracted and very well aware of it, but our relationship remained limited. I mean, there was always a point at which we would let go sexually and then stop. That's probably not so different than lots of other women with repressed backgrounds, growing up in a Catholic background with an overprotective father. Then I also had a very good friend whom I dated all through college who was a very nice man, but it was very nonsexual. He was my friend. I could be me, and it was just a very beautiful friendship.

Then I moved to New York City. Coming from a sheltered all-girls school, living in New York City was a trauma. The whole year was a trauma, both in finding a place to live and just in finding my identity, period. That was very much a crucial turning point. I would cry for weeks at a time. I very, very strongly considered suicide. I was also going through my rebellion of giving up religion, finding there was nothing of religious value that made any sense, and there's just no meaning in life. My sexual development went a little further, but it was often very traumatic because it was not like natural relationships blossoming; it was often meeting someone and having a one night stand—very unfulfilling.

What were you doing there?

I was working. My job was good, I enjoyed my job. I worked at a Foster Care Agency, foster care and adoption. I was a social worker and giving to other people was very, very fulfilling. One interesting experience was that I had a girl in my caseload then who was seventeen and had a hand exactly like mine. She was assigned to my very purposely. Of course than I was only twenty-two or something, and that was very difficult. I knew the pain she was going through, but I wasn't together enough to help her with it. It was just too close to home to deal with. She seemed to be a constant reflection of the pain I was in somehow.

But then I went to grad school in Chicago after that. Graduate school was a place where I began to find myself. Things started coming together. That was where I got into therapy. I think that helped. I really dealt with my sexual identity for the first time. I was starting to let in how repressed I was, and how unfulfilled I felt in every area, particularly as a woman.

Well, for my sexual development, the first person I had intercourse with was a black man who was a very lovely person, but we didn't really share a lot in common. We had a very sexual relationship, but it was sort of painfully sexual because my sexual identity was still very fragmented. In many ways, this man was quite delightful and I would have liked to have integrated him into my life, but I couldn't for many reasons.

Then I got into a relationship that was very, very important to me with a man who was quite a bit older than I. Our relationship was superb and I lived with him for many years very much in love. He really helped me a lot with my body image, my sexuality. I grew constantly and it was like I saw myself flowering as a person. But I think the choice of an older person must have again been in some way still a piece of this fragmentation somewhere.

My image as a woman at that point began to flourish and I got into Jungian analysis which centered around what being a woman and being a creative being meant to me. They were very interrelated. At that level the exploration became more fun because it wasn't always pain. But I always was so totally aware that deep, deep down ultimately I didn't value myself. I considered myself ugly. However, I knew I could go home to this man and have him validate me in some way, remind me that I had some attractive features and remind me that I was fairly intelligent. I just really didn't believe those things somehow. I had confidence in myself at some level, but there was still this existential crisis that was gnawing. So what happened is I left Chicago.

All this related to my identity as a disabled person, because until that time I still had not really dealt with it. I began to deal with it in my relationship with this man because he is a very creative, artistic person, did his own photography and was just really fun. We would do things like take pictures of each other, of my whole body, including my hand, and up to that point I would never allow myself before a camera. It really helped me as a sexual person as well; it began to make me like my body. I began to look at myself as an art form. It seems I had to abstract myself that way in order to deal with it.

I terminated the relationship even though it was going very well, basically because I knew that I had to totally get away from it to see if I could like and accept myself and if I could be a positive person without a man sitting next to me reassuring me.

Losses came to me one after another right then. My father died very suddenly, the day after I put in my resignation to come back to Boston. I was coming back, with this vague sense of crisis, or transition, because what I came to find out was whether or not I could somehow be happy, you know, and like myself, without being validated by others. I knew that loss was the name of the game, somehow. That I had to like loss or understand it in some way. And I did. Somehow, I dropped all the other defenses and began to realize the real loss, or a very crucial loss, that I had to deal with was my hand and what that meant.

That's when I began looking for a new job related to disability. I realized that what I really wanted to do was to be involved with the growth of people with disabilities.

But no job around satisfied me, so I had to create my own.

I understand you've been involved with the disability rights movement. Is this related?

Yes, a friend and I developed and ran groups for people with disabilities. Although we designed them to help people explore personal issues around living with disabilities, we found ourselves making lists of concrete problems in society which needed changing. As the groups continued, many people began to see them as a basis for mutual support and advocacy.

"I" became a "We." I experienced others' pain in being dif-

ferent. We realized that collectively we could bring about
changes in our own lives and for others. To me, the disability
movement means the right to have and express a positive identity.
Each of us must choose that identity.

So, several of us, all with disabilities, created a Self Help
Center for counseling and advocacy. I quit my job and became
the center's director. All of us had questions about the medical
model of service. We evolved alternative strategies. This
philosophy made it harder to get money from traditional sources.
But after a while, our effectiveness spoke for itself and we got a
grant.

After the money came through, I was offered a job teaching
about Section 504 to various audiences, including consumer
groups around the country.

I had worked at the Center for over a year without any income. I was burned out. I realized that I had let many of my own
good qualities be devalued again. I had put my professional skills
and talents into the Center. And my experiences with a disability.
It was hard being poor for a year.

Without realizing it, I had become a victim of the cause I
believed in. I was embarrassed by my professionalism, and about
my need for not being poor. Being a rational, effective administrator seemed as though I had "sold out." When I accepted
the consultant job, I did it because of the importance of 504. It
also showed my right to a professional status. I began to realize
that I was not selling out, but was fighting for the same cause
only in a different way where I could apply what I knew about
society, money, political activity and all the rest, to help get 504
implemented.

What does Section 504 mean to you?

Section 504 means a lot to me. It says to able-bodied people
that disabled people have rights too. They have the rights to participate in programs that the able-bodied have had for years.
They have the right to determine their own limitations and
strengths. 504 says that the disabled have civil rights too.

504 is liberating. It helps disabled people and able-bodied
people to understand that we are in charge of our own lives.
There are many disabled people — together we are powerful. We
have the right and obligation to define our place as contributing

members of society. For the first time, under 504, our lives are placed in our own hands. For the first time, we are something more than the creation of others. We can see ourselves as positive. If we insist that we have something to contribute and we belong, eventually able-bodied people will have to acknowledge us. If we doubt ourselves, other people will doubt us too and perpetuate our precariousness and insecurity.

Section 504 is a civil rights law. It protects our freedom to participate in all social institutions and services which receive certain kinds of federal money.

504 has helped me to wake up and see myself as a creative person who has rights. 504 has helped me to see my disability and my limitations in a broader perspective. That is, I am a human being first. I have many strengths and weaknesses and my disability is one. I have to use my own experience to show other people my limits and strengths. I choose how to focus my disability. I flow with it and merge into the fullness of my being.

504 has helped me recognize that disability is neither a positive nor a negative thing. It just is. And so, what other people think about it no longer makes me powerless.

Of course, Section 504 is not going to be implemented without disabled people pushing for it all around. For that matter, disabled people have to push for a lot of legislation — on the books and not yet on the books. 504 tells able-bodied people to question their own actions and, for that matter, their own weaknesses and chances of becoming disabled. Disabled people know how hard these kinds of thoughts are. But we should not be the shields taking all the flack for helping people deal with some realities.

For me, Section 504 is liberation in the making. It has helped me make sense of who I am and where I am. It has helped me realize that I am a creative and dignified human being.

Don Berry

What goes into the rehabilitation of a person newly disabled? What happens when it becomes apparent that the disability is permanent? And what happens if the disabled person should desire to live independently? Most decisions about a disabled person are made for that person. Abraham Lincoln's characterization of the American experiment as a government of the people by the people and for the people is misplaced for while policy may be designed for the disabled it is rarely designed by them. There is much reason why it should be.

The different body that distinguishes a disabled person from an able-bodied one is disclosed through its many and complex relationships with the physical and social environment. While professionals know much about these relationships, it is demanding the impossible to expect that they know everything. What professional should reasonably be expected to know that Don Berry did not want an elaborate wheelchair? Why were channels of communication not opened to Don regarding the sort of catheterization that he was to have? And why are disabled people outside of the hospital environment still treated *instead of being allowed a voice in fashioning their own lives, the environment in which their lives will be lived, and the public policy that will influence them?*

Many of the interviews in this book lament the actions of professionals. Of course there are many times, particularly at the outset of the life of a person as disabled, when professional wisdom should be relied on. At the beginning the case is likely to be largely medical, perhaps an emergency where the professional is the only one who knows what is to be done. But surely, as life

36

goes on, as emergency subsides, decisions are made otherwise. Why can they not be made with *the person involved? Disabled people tend to be aware of the needs of their own bodies and of the benefits of professional wisdom. Here dialogue is likely to benefit the physical well being of the disabled person.*

But there is more. For experiences at the beginning are important during the rest of life. If decisions are here dictated unilaterally, it may be hard for the handicapped person to make other decisions in the long run. The ability to make decisions on one's own is something one expects from any adult. Not to expect it of a disabled person is to treat that person as a child. In no small measure the independence that Don and other handicapped people speak of is the independence to make decisions for themselves. Such decisions may well involve the advice of professionals. But the ultimate power over one's own life, as with the able-bodied adult, must rest with the disabled person.

With the power to make decisions comes the chance of mistakes, the responsibility for mistakes and for one's whole life. Responsibility breeds dignity. Exercised with professionals when needed and without them when they are unnecessary, it is part of the social recovery of the handicapped person.

As in private so in public. Handicapped people have started to claim a greater voice in the policy that traditionally has been shaped by others. Again, practically, there is good reason why they should: most able-bodied persons are not sensitive to issues like curb cuts or braille markings. (Such sensitivity usually only comes after the fact, which makes the realization of policy not only important in and of itself but for symbolic reasons as well.) The able-bodied person may not realize the snags in the welfare system making it difficult for a disabled person to work, or what the disabled person may need in the ways of an education—and the frequently only minor program modifications that make an education possible. Disabled people realize these things because they live with them.

Disabled people should have a part in articulating the policy that affects them. Once again, however, there is more here than issues of practicality, aptness, and physical and social need. As well there is the issue of adulthood, of citizenship. For a disabled person to be a citizen in this country means the right and the obligation to make significant decisions affecting his or her life. Frequently this is more obligation than opportunity. Yet it is an obligation that society at large has a right to impose on those disabled people who expect alterations in that society. Most of the people speaking in these pages wish such an obligation.

When I was 18 years old, I had a swelling in my spine that damaged the nervous system, causing paralysis and rendering me a paraplegic. Transverse myelitis is the general name of my disability; they don't really know the cause. It could have been caused by a blow to the back or a virus or any number of things. Functionally it means not being able to do a lot of the things that I would normally be able to do, like walking or climbing stairs. It also means having to depend on others for assistance. A lot of the physical things that I used to do I can't do anymore. There is also the psychological aspect to deal with.

Did your disability have a gradual or sudden onset?

I was at a drive-in with my girlfriend. We were just watching the movie and I started getting sharp pains in my back, and they started getting worse. I felt as if I was going to pass out or something. So I had her go up to the snack bar and call my parents to come and pick me up, because I didn't know what was wrong. She went to get help, but I felt I couldn't wait, so I went up to the snack bar. I was afraid. It was all so painful, and I was scared because I didn't know what was going on. I was perspiring and everything. On the way up to the snack bar, I was staggering like I was drunk, and I was aware of people yelling at me because I was banging into their cars. I got up to the snack bar and it was closed, so I knocked on the door and kept knocking until somebody finally answered. I told them that I thought I was going to pass out and they let me come in to wait for my parents.

Did you have any fears that you were dying?

No, not at that time. I just sat down in a chair, and then I decided that I should lie down on the floor. I started to get down and couldn't move my legs. That scared me. I stayed there for about 15 minutes, until my parents got there, and they immediately called the hospital and an ambulance came. By then I couldn't move anything, my arms or my legs.

I do remember one kind of funny thing. I could barely breathe at the time, and my Dad was going to give me artificial respiration and I refused it—I thought it was kind of a silly idea. He didn't give it to me but the ambulance came right after that and I was given oxygen and taken to the hospital.

Once I got there, I was passing out and only remember parts of it—waking in the x-ray room, seeing spinal fluid go down to a certain point and then stop and hearing them say this was where the swelling was, waking up in Intensive Care later while they were doing a tracheotomy and seeing all these faces around me. I didn't know what was going on and when I did wake up for a few minutes and see these things I was scared, and then I would pass out again. It was like this for a couple of days. When I came out of it I was on a breathing machine in Intensive Care. In the next couple of days they called my parents down twice and told them if they wanted to see me they had better come, that I was dying (I found this out later). After that time I was just worried—about my parents worrying, and about myself, because I didn't know if I was going to die or what.

At that time I couldn't even move my head. And at first I couldn't talk. That was really frustrating because I couldn't communicate at all. Then, eventually, if someone put their finger over the tracheotomy, I could get words out, barely. There were things I wanted to ask, and things I wanted to say, and I couldn't. It took so long just to make a simple sentence or ask a question that I became so frustrated that I didn't want to talk. It made me realize the communication problems that people with things like real heavy cerebral palsy have. If a person loses his arms and legs, well, you can still communicate if you have to; but if you lose both, and also your means of communicating, this makes it very difficult.

When did you reach the point where you realized you weren't going to get better?

In the first hospital there was a guy who had broken his neck and he was all right after a bunch of therapy. I figured spinal cord injuries were all the same, that I would be like him. And there was a guy in my room that I knew and went to high school with who had broken his neck and he was all right. After a month or two he got up and left with no problems at all. I figured that I would be recovering over a long period of time. That is what the doctors had told me, too, that it would take a long time to get better. First they said a short time, then they said a long time. I was recovering and I figured they were right, because I was getting more movement all the time.

Then I sort of realized that they had been saying *well* for a year or two, and after that they said you will get *better*. But I was not getting any better any more. I wasn't recovering as fast as I thought I should, so I started figuring that I wouldn't get better. Then I transferred to the next hospital and saw a lot of other disabled people who weren't recovering even years after spinal cord injury. At that point I didn't want to face it, but I knew down deep that I wasn't going to get any better.

They didn't tell me that I wasn't going to get better for the longest time, it was almost like they were putting it off. Maybe at first they didn't know. Maybe they figured that when the swelling went down (they didn't know what caused it anyway) I would recover. I really don't know.

How did you feel about the care you received?

As I look back at the whole time I was in the hospital, I was resentful and angry at the lack of knowledge they had — not the lack of knowledge, but the lack of using what they did have. For example, with catheterization, I know that they knew the difference between how a bladder could function with or without a catheter. And I know that when I was in the hospital a woman came and explained it, and one time they tried me without an indwelling catheter and my bladder worked, I just couldn't control it. They had external catheters which people used for drainage and I could have used one of those, but they made me keep the indwelling catheter, and I didn't know the difference. I accepted what they said as truth. As a result, I ended up with a lot of unnecessary infections and I was sick a lot. I went home one Christmas and some urine leaked out from around the side of the catheter, and it scared us, because they hadn't explained that this could happen. I bet you that it's easier to put a person on an indwelling catheter than it is to have to change a leg bag and deal with that [an external catheter]. I resent lots of things that happened.

What other ways could the hospital staff have helped?

I hardly ever saw or talked with my doctor. An aide used to come by and check me. I think it would have been a lot more helpful for me to talk to the doctor and have him explain all the aspects of my disability and how I could function in my daily life with it. Maybe the doctors didn't know about independent living. But even if they didn't, they should have tried to get me off the catheter and give a lot of counseling to me and my family.

They should have classes for people who are disabled to inform them about their disability and what it means. They never explained anything; then they said, "Well, you will be paralyzed." But even then they didn't say what they meant. They didn't say I wouldn't be able to move but would have all my feeling, or I wouldn't have any feeling — you know, what does it mean? They didn't even say anything to my family, which caused us a lot of worry and grief, just from lack of knowledge. When a doctor came in to tell me (finally) that I wasn't going to walk, I was in a ward — you know there are six beds in a ward — and there were other people around. I felt sorry for him because he was nervous, stuttering, and everything else, and he could hardly tell me anything.

A doctor should tell people about alternatives and the options that they have — schooling, jobs, etc. Show people how they can live independently, how they can set up their home, how the family can make it easier for the person in the wheelchair to live independently.

They had me doing occupational therapy, making a sliding board, which is a board (it can be any length) that you put half under you and half on the bed or on the car seat and you slide over instead of having people lift you. You can do it yourself. They figured it was good therapy for my arms and hands to work on the sliding board by the sanding (that was while I was getting physical therapy to build up my arms). They could have taught me other things but they didn't. And I was there nine months.

It was nice to make the sliding board, I still have it, but it didn't do me any good as far as learning how to do any of the essentials involved in daily living. There was a whole lot of other things that would have been more beneficial. They could have taught me how to cook, how to get in and out of a car, how to go to the bathroom and empty the leg bag myself, how to do personal care—the easiest way to take your shirt off—any number of the things a person needs to do in everyday life. I don't know why they didn't. Maybe they were under the impression that as a paraplegic I would be living in an institution, or with my family, or something to that effect, for the rest of my life and that I wouldn't need to know these things.

An example of poor judgment is when the physical therapist at the hospital ordered me a wheelchair. You can order wheelchairs any way you want them, and instead of ordering me a standard wheelchair they ordered me one that was incredibly impractical. It had little wheels on it, it was wider and longer than the standard wheelchair, it had a high recliner on the back of it with a zipper down the back, and everything you could think of on a wheelchair. Plus it had bright royal blue upholstery. If you are disabled and you don't like the idea of being disabled anyway, and you feel conspicuous being in a wheelchair, and then they put you in a chair that has fins and sticks out like a sore thumb, you feel even more conspicuous.

At first I felt the doctors were experts and that they knew what they were talking about. I accepted their word as law, but as time went on I started learning things from observing others who were disabled and talking with them. I probably learned more from other people in wheelchairs than I did from any of the doctors. If you never see a doctor but once every two weeks and they just come by to see how you are feeling, and you are lying there and cannot move, and can't do anything, and obviously you're not sick, but you feel rotten—and then they leave and go on their rounds—the doctor is not doing you a whole lot of good. He may have the knowledge to put you into therapy or something, but as far as his saying, "Look here, let me help you," he doesn't help you at all. I have no confidence in doctors, and I didn't all through the therapy while I was there. So I learned very little from doctors.

But I learned a lot from physical therapists, because I had good relationships with them. Physically, I learned how to lift weights. That was good, but I think physical therapy helped me more because of the relationship of talking and having the feeling that somebody actually cared (even though some of it was false, because they go to that job and they have to act nice). You go there and at least there is a friendly face, somebody that you can be with half of the day. Then they leave at night, and that is a completely different story.

There was nobody to talk to about our problems and nobody qualified to deal with our problems at night. There were three other guys my age, we were 19 or 20 at the time, and we just sat around and drank. We didn't have anything else to do in the hospital. We would go up into a room or down to one of the floors and we would get a fifth and some 7-Up—like one fifth and one bottle of 7-up and we would drink it. We would do this, like, three nights a week, and that is how we spent our evenings. At five o'clock all the friendly faces go home, the therapists and everybody go home and you are left (unless friends come up to visit you, and I was up in a new area and didn't know anybody except the people I had met in the hospital) to find your own entertainment. Once in a while they would have a Bingo game, but at that time I certainly wasn't enthusiastic about playing Bingo.

Dinner was at four-thirty or five and that left us up at night with nothing to do. We wanted to do things. We didn't just want to watch TV every night. But we couldn't leave the hospital, we had no transportation. Even if the hospital had a transportation van it doesn't mean they would have taken us out in the evenings.

Would it be possible to set up a hospital where there would be things to do besides playing Bingo and getting drunk?

I think they could. On weekends they should have *small* groups go somewhere. They have enough staff for this. When a person is newly disabled you are leery of being around other people with disabilities and you don't like to go out in groups, to the movies, or to the zoo or wherever they want to take you. You know, a group of 15 wheelchairs tromping around—I don't like it to this day, and I won't go on things like that.

How did your family react to your disability?

After my stay in the hospital I went home for five months. It was hard on the whole family, an adjustment that took a great deal of time. Part of it was our lack of knowledge of services and programs available, the uncertainty of just how independent I could be. For example, it took my parents months before they felt comfortable in leaving me alone for an overnight. It was almost like I was a child again.

In any case, it was difficult at home, because I became too dependent on my family. If you're there, and become too dependent and ask for all your needs, your home life can become a strain. I wanted to do something else, but I didn't know what. People told me about a rehab hospital with a wing for young people. I went with one other guy and stayed for three months. There were young people coming in, but after the three months they decided finally that they couldn't really put up with young people. They started to tell me, when I would go out on a date and come in real late, like 2:30, to try and come in by 11:00, before the nurses change shifts, so there would be someone to help me into bed and make it easier for the evening shift. I was going out with one of the aides who had worked there, and I finally left because of the restrictions and moved into an apartment with her. Since then I have always lived independently.

Was living independently a big adjustment?

To get out into the real world you have to be able to accept your disability in the sense that you want to put up with numerous obstacles — finding an apartment that you can get into and can get around in, finding a way to shop, etc. You can stay in a nursing home or stay with your parents and have most of those needs taken care of. But, your parents won't always be there, and a nursing home is not the ideal place; it's worse than a hospital. I think that a person has to psychologically accept his disability and be ready to want to do other things besides worrying about a disability. That's when people start wanting to go to school or to live out or try something new besides whatever is safe and secure.

Tell me about the Catch-22 of work and welfare dependence.

Well, you go through vocational rehabilitation and training programs with the ultimate goal of obtaining a job. But, you get through all your training and the problem is that you have to find a job that pays enough, because, as a paraplegic you have to pay for attendants and you have to pay for medical supplies — all the extra needs that the nondisabled person doesn't have. I have to hire people to help me up in the morning and help me into bed at night, and to do the cooking, cleaning, whatever. And most nondisabled people don't have to do that. You also have to buy certain medical supplies, which are outrageous in price. For the nondisabled person these are nonexistent expenses.

The way it is now, you complete all this training and you secure a job, but it doesn't pay enough. If you had stayed on welfare you could have received your maximum of, say, $450 for attendant care and $235 for SSI—that's all tax free and you have your medical and dental supplies paid for. So, you've got the training, but you can't find a job that pays enough to enable you to get off welfare. A lot of people could find a job almost equal to what they get on benefits, but they don't want it. Why should they work eight hours a day for less than they are making by not working at all?

It would be really great if the welfare system was structured in such a way that the people who are receiving the welfare can turn around and work whatever hours they are physically able to work, in volunteer programs or programs of their choice, and call that their jobs. Turn around and say, "There you are, employed for $800 a month, to work for as many hours as you can in these programs," instead of "Here's $400 a month" or $800 (whatever a person gets for welfare). A lot of people can't work full time, or they can't work at all because of disability. But the ones who can and want to be employed should be given the opportunity. There's a lot of people that want to work and get off welfare, but they can't afford to, literally. If there were a system where I could have a job plus, say my attendant needs of $400 or whatever a month, and if I could find a job like any other person and have that $400 supplement, then I would be willing to work because then I would be on the same scale as everybody else.

How important is it for disabled people to have some say in the structure of services available to the disabled?

I think it is vital. Disabled people should have input into any of the programs that are for their own benefit, because they know their needs; otherwise, some essential programs—like transportation—may be omitted. The nondisabled policymaker may forget altogether that if you're in a wheelchair you can't get into a bus, or you need an elevator or a lift onto it. Often people in a bureaucracy don't know of the need and are not willing to work for and push programs that are not directly connected with them. Say there's 500,000 people in wheelchairs and there's 10,000,000 people not in wheelchairs. Well, it's a lot easier for the people making the programs to have no concern or direct involvement with the disabled. Then they'll say "Well, let's make a transportation system that will fit the majority of the people."

But it's not only the omission of many programs, it is the idea that disabled people should have some control over what kind of processes rule their lives. I'd rather have some choice in what I do and what kind of options I want for my life, than have somebody tell me what to do. I'd rather have the choice of having input into a program, and knowing the benefits of the different choices. A disabled person, not only by input but by his physical being, can provide a role model for other disabled people. And it also shows nondisabled that disabled people are not all in nursing homes, or timid individuals.

What do you think of the clichés, such as "Hire the Handicapped"?

It's a push to give people jobs, but ineffective overall. There are so many slogans around, that it's just like any other sign that people look at. I don't like the word "handicapped." Labels like "handicapped" or "crippled," or "invalid," etc., are a hindrance to the disabled movement. A person must have some self-respect, and if you consider yourself "crippled" it's almost like considering yourself a negative concept. If I have to be stigmatized and classified, then I would prefer to be called disabled, for the simple reason that I am unable to do a number of things. But I am really against any classification.

What about the cliché, "God, isn't it a pity, that handsome young man..."?

People say things like that. You just have to ignore them. You can say, "Yeah, isn't it a pity God allows pollution?" or "Isn't it a pity God allows war?" You can say, "Isn't it a pity George Washington didn't live forever?" or something like that. People who say those clichés may feel sorry, and it's too bad; if they actually knew me they probably wouldn't feel sorry for me.

What about "Gee, he's so brave..."?

Brave for what? Brave because you've accepted your disability? It's something that happened that you eventually learn to live with. It's the same as a person who gets acne and has scars left over from it: "Gee, a person is brave because he lives with those scars." A lot of these things are just worthless sayings that you just ignore or tolerate. People just react, they don't know what else to say. Much of it is ignorance, and you either listen to it or try to change people's attitudes. For so many years and for so long disabled people have not been seen, and the only exposure that people receive is from television programs that have the disabled with emotional, psychological and other kind of problems along with their disability. Or, they're unreal. So the exposure that people have had is incorrect and inaccurate.

If you had that magic wand to change the world around, what changes would you make?

All the blind would like to see, all the disabled would like to walk, whatever they may say. I did it before and I know what it's like, but it's not going to be like that anymore and I can't really do a whole lot about it. So, I deal with my life as it is now. When people talk about certain things and their experiences they had that I can't do now, I know what they're talking about because I have experienced a lot of those. Some of them I haven't, and some of them I wouldn't if I was walking. But I do know a lot of experiences that a person who has been disabled all their lives may not. Sometimes it also affects me in the sense that I become angry when I can't do something. But there's a lot of things people want that they can't have, and that's the way it is.

It's a hypothetical question and I don't have the power to make those changes so there's no point in speculating. I can't change my disability, but I can and do maximize my independence and try and change the attitude and stereotypes of people I come into contact with. I just go on with my life and enjoy it. I have a disability, but it's not the main factor in my life anymore.

Nancy Kaye

Nancy Kaye is a female university professor who is handicapped. She may be angry. She surely wants some things changed. Perhaps anger in the face of injustice is entirely reasonable.

Nancy has things to say about Public Law 94-142, the Education for All Handicapped Children Act. This law has been and will be controversial. Nancy adds to the controversy the views of a handicapped professional and handicapped child now a handicapped adult. On Nancy's part these views are considered; perhaps we as a society should consider them as well before concluding that decent education for handicapped children is too expensive, too difficult, too much of a burden.

Public Law 94-142 and sections 503 and 504 of the Rehabilitation Act of 1973 are milestones in the history of handicapped people. As with any public policy there is a gap between the policy and its implementation. Part of the gap is the difficulty of constructing organizations for implementation; part is the costs or perceived costs of the policy. Only marginally, I believe, is it related to the malevolence of some people—ignorance perhaps, malevolence no.

Both acts only promise to handicapped people rights that able-bodied citizens of this nation have long taken for granted. To the able-bodied, then, they may be trivial. To the disabled, just because they offer inclusion instead of exclusion, they are anything but trivial.

Vigorous enforcement is necessary to the handicapped. And morally, it is necessary to the able-bodied.

A word about the question of cost: first, in the short term at

49

least, it is a very real question. Second, any policy which provides for improvement in the lives of so many is costly. And third we don't really know what the net costs will be. In fact, in the longer run, they promise to be less than they now appear. Strong arguments can be made that they are more cost beneficial than the alternatives of institutionalization, dead-end special education, vocational rehabilitation for nonexistent jobs, and countless other programs.

In Nancy's case much of the intent of such public policy was realized privately. She comes from a wealthy background; her father was a physician. She had the best of medical care; her father was able to exact respect.

Nancy says the chances of making it "being poor are very, very small." She goes on to say that the chances of making it if one is also handicapped are "almost zero." This is one of those propositions in social science that seem reasonable but require demonstration. If, in fact, true it might be that a prudent sort of social policy would be to increase the resources in money and kind available to handicapped children. To insure against the event of becoming handicapped or of having a handicapped child may be desirable, particularly given a society which makes having a disability most undesirable. Since handicapped children can occur in any family, and since we all can become disabled, there is a strong insurance aspect to such support which may make it attractive to an able-bodied society which thinks realistically about the probabilities of handicap. As "making it" means in part contributing to society, such an endeavor, even if costly, may well be cost-beneficial.

I'm a mother, woman, professional, activist — probably in that order. I'm also a compulsive over-achiever, a "doer," and I'm learning to just "be." My whole life has been doing instead of just being. Ever since I can remember I was always doing something, and always felt that if I wasn't doing something then I wasn't worthwhile. It was not okay to just kind of lay back. That has really struck me in the last month since I had an operation for a kidney infection. I don't know how to recover from surgery. I'm either sick or I'm well, and this transition time...

I have spina bifida, which is a congenital deformity of the spinal column. Because I spent so many years in bed I've had a number of kidney stones. My legs are only partially paralyzed, but I get more handicapped because I have these other issues to deal with, a kidney infection, a bladder infection, a loss of circulation, trophic ulcers. All of these are manifestations of my handicap.

I was sick for several weeks after surgery. Then when I started to feel better the first thing that I thought about doing was going back to work, because if I'm not sick, obviously I should be doing something. Yet, my body is saying I'm not healed enough. I look okay and I'm ambulating better than I was; I certainly sit at a desk at work. But I have chosen to go through the process of recovery, and now I'm learning how to pay attention to what my body is saying. I've had a lot of anxiety about it though, not pushing myself into work.

What's the difference between being sick and having a handicap?

In my family and in my language system being sick is a flare-up, a result of my handicap. It is not being able to do what I am normally able to do. Although I am handicapped all of the time I am still able to work, talk, think, drive a car, keep house, take care of my kid, go to the show. Being sick is not being able to do that. It's a degree on a continuum. It's the other side of being handicapped. Only more severe.

What is the extent of your physical handicap?

Well, my legs have never been paralyzed where I've not been able to move them at all. But I've had to spend time in a wheelchair when I was not able to use my legs. So I've been slipping back and forth between a wheelchair, crutches, and walking. I didn't walk until I was twenty-four, sixteen years ago, so before that it was just between crutches and a wheelchair. For a long time I thought this bouncing around made me phenomenally schizophrenic. In my head, I am very close to normal when I am walking. Now I know I don't walk like other people, but in my head it feels like I am walking like other people. And I am doing the things that other people are doing: walking, carrying my own things, getting up from the chair without help, etc. But when I'm on crutches I am more handi-

capped than normal and when I'm in a wheelchair I am handicapped. And I can do that within the course of a day. I did my walking this morning and felt really good and normal, then took my daughter for her driver's license exam and was in a wheelchair and felt very handicapped, and then I came over here on crutches.

I hear you saying that there is some kind of equation in your mind between handicap-badness and walking-goodness.

No. The difference in feeling normal to handicapped is in the degree of ambulation: Handicap equals constraint and walking equals freedom. I don't feel that I'm handicapped when I am teaching, for example, and I do that sitting down. But I don't have that sense of being constrained and not being able to move.

Do you think of yourself as being a handicapped person or a person with a handicap?

A person with a handicap. The description "handicapped person" means that the handicap is paramount, overrides the person. "A person with a handicap" implies, for me, something else, there's something else here—I'm also a person with red hair, a person who is right-handed, a person who is Jewish, a person who is white, a person who is female. For a long time I believed I was a handicapped person. And that was the only thing I had going for or against me. And it's simply not true any longer. I know it affects relationships and style of interaction, my view of the world, but so does being female. And I'm not always sure which has more of an impact, being female or handicapped.

What is the relationship between your being female and being handicapped?

I don't remember being raised as a female child. I've read a lot about how female children are raised versus male children. And I'm not sure that that was a consideration when I was little. As a teenager it became real important and I was real, real scared that I was not going to be a female, I was only going to be handicapped. I spent two agonizing years waiting to menstruate. Of course I didn't have the information and so I thought that because I was handicapped I wasn't going to menstruate, I wasn't going to get breasts, and I wasn't going to develop; I was just going to be one of these neuter cripples wandering around. But then I did start to menstruate and I did start to develop a female body, and for a while there was a relaxation of that whole issue of being handicapped. When I started to go out with males that handicapped female thing came up again. It was almost like the handicapped person part of me couldn't allow "normal" things to happen. It was interesting that the first man I loved, the one I married — our style of interaction was for me to perform.

I met him when I was fifteen, and in a way he challenged me to do some things that were really kind of neat. But some of the underlying messages were, at least I felt that they were, Look at all the things you're doing and you're handicapped! It wasn't like, Look at all the things you're doing because females do this or people do it. I often describe it as feeling like an ornament on a Christmas tree, and he kind of plunked me on his arm and showed me off: Look at my girlfriend who did this or who did that, but you have to look at her to realize that there's something else there. Now, well I guess I've spent the last twenty years trying to resolve that. I haven't arrived yet, I'm still in the process, but I'm much stronger in terms of believing that I am a woman who has a handicap.

My marriage was a growing up point. I felt that if I got married the next day I'd be a rose. There would be some kind of magic when I became Mrs. Then there wasn't and it was a terrible disappointment and it was no different than the day before in terms of how I felt about myself or how I felt about my husband. When I had my first date I thought, Well I must not be that crippled, because here's this good looking young man who finds me attractive. My marriage said to me that I was less handicapped than I thought I was, because I was able to hook a man. Having a baby made me even less handicapped because I was able to fulfill one of the female roles in society and was really rewarded for it. And my divorce, I guess, was also a real landmark in terms of creating who I am today.

There are some things that I have to deal with as a woman with a handicap that other nonhandicapped women would not deal with. I am more woman now than I am handicapped, and feel really good about that. I don't get really flipped out anymore by guys who think it would be real interesting to sleep with a cripple. I don't know if there are a lot like that but I sure met my fair share. That's something that I'm much more able to deal with now that I ever was before. I never talked to another handicapped woman about that kind of thing and when I have talked about other women's sexuality that is not a dimension that they can relate to.

I don't know any women with handicaps that I could talk to about it. I know women who have handicaps but we are not friends. I know them professionally or have met them at various places. At this point in time I've met two, three people with handicaps since I've moved here. So it's circumstances rather than anything else. If I found one I think I would talk. I have talked to male friends about it, and asked them if they thought I was crazy for believing it, and one admitted that that was one of the strongest attractions when he first met me. Now it's okay cause we can talk about it, but it was not okay in the beginning cause I really sensed it.

What are the differences between being a handicapped man and a handicapped woman?

In our society the man is the one who is supposed to be the aggressor, and take care of everything. And handicap means that you don't do that. I could play the female role, the traditional feminine role in our society and be accepted both as a female and as handicapped because they are very similar. You're passive and you're kind and you're nurturing and you don't get angry and those kinds of things. I have not played that role, so that's caused a real dissonance between role expectations and what I'm laying out, but I think that with the handicapped male the dissonance in terms of gender and handicap is immediately apparent. I mean the question is, how can you be macho and handicapped? That's kind of, I think, the ultimate dissonance in terms of men.

What was it like for you growing up? Is there anything you would have changed?

If I could change, if I could start all over again, but keep all the good things that I like about me, then the thing I would change is being handicapped. No, I guess I wouldn't change anything, since I like who I am today and it's the sum total of everything that I've lived through.

I had a very, very, strong, caring group of people. I grew up believing that I was an okay human being, okay being translated to mean that everybody has things that you like about them and that you don't like, and your shit smells, but that's still okay, cause that's what makes you human. Lots of doubts about self over the years, but my humaness was still a central theme.

I don't think the term "handicapped" was ever used in my house. As a child I knew I was different, but that difference never made me feel less human or less worthwhile. I didn't start school until I was eleven. Up until that time I stayed at home or in a hospital. I had home teaching. Nearly everybody that I came in contact with, the real significant people in my life, loved me and cared about me as a human being, so I was not made to feel subhuman. As I ventured out into the real world, I got lots of messages about being handicapped, but I had such a strong basis by that time that, while it got shaken at times, it was never destroyed.

Oh, I would have liked to have been in the mainstream a heck of a lot sooner than I was. And it's not really a regret, it's more of a sadness around missing things. I would have liked to have been able to go on picnics, and, you know, explore and so on. It's a contradiction, I would have liked to have been able to do it earlier, but then I might have gotten those other kinds of messages. But I still would have liked to have gone out earlier to see what the world was like.

My father was a physician and was financially comfortable. I wouldn't be alive if there weren't those resources that allowed my family the option of devoting time to me as opposed to trying to find shelter or food. Mother had a maid, and we had a chauffer and a laundress, so the primary amount of time was spent with the children as opposed to survival. Those resources make a significant difference. My father could afford to have round the clock nurses and to call in any specialist that would be necessary and to give any kind of medication because he had the money. The chances of making it being poor are very, very small. And then when you're handicapped it's almost zero. It would take a phenomenal effort to be able to pull yourself out of both.

What does "making it" mean?

For one thing, just on the sheer physical level, being able to live and get the proper kind of medication and treatment that one would need. If physical survival is not an issue, then "making it" would be to realize one's potential. I'm sure that there are many children who were excluded from school or given damaging messages, the result being that their aspiration level was dramatically reduced from what it should have been or could have been. We do that as a society rather well to all poor folks. And then to be handicapped as well... It's a devastating combination. You have to have money in order to acquire the resources that are necessary for handicapped people to develop and cope — to survive; yet being handicapped drains resources.

As far as my handicap, my father took over; he was the sole depository of information and he made all of the decisions. My mother was like an inactive observer. She knew nothing about what was happening to me or what was "wrong" with me. After my father died she transferred the role that he played to my physician, and my physician played that role. I have very clear memories of that relationship between my surgeon and my mother. He gave her bits of information. In fact, my sister and brother had lots of misconceptions about what was going on with me as a child because my mother never shared anything with them. My mother has not been involved, really, until this recent operation. By involved I mean at an understanding and emotional level; a place where my mother could understand where I was at and I could understand where she was at, a place where we could share our fears and mutually support each other.

So what changed?

I decided that I wanted to work on changing my behavior related to my handicap and being "sick." I entered therapy with that contract. Obviously I was not just a single entity doing this, it had to do with how I interact with my daughter, my mother, friends, and a whole range of things. I think I wound up having surgery when I did so I could test it all out and try out behaviors that I had not tried out before, like asking for help, sharing my fears with my mother. The first time my mother has ever seen me cry during any kind of hospitalization or illness since I was very small was this time. My family and I now talk and analyze feelings.

For example, my sister, who I've spent a lot of time talking to, has usually felt guilt as her first reaction. This is because she feels too healthy and has a sister she loves who is not healthy. Then she has a reaction about being totally helpless, that there isn't anything she can do. This of course exaggerates the guilt. If she could only do something then she wouldn't feel so guilty. I contribute to her feelings because when I call her and she says "If you want, I will come," I do a "Wonder Woman" number and say, "No. You don't need to. I'll be able to take care of it." This time, however, I realized that I needed and wanted support. I wanted my sister so I decided to call her, share my fears, and ask her to come. Before I had a chance to do that my sister called me back and said, "I'm coming to be with you because I want to be there and I want to support you and unless you bar the door I am going to arrive at such and such a time." And so that was really neat because we had both come to the same conclusion. When I picked her up at the airport I felt really, really good because I was getting support for me. She is very caring and very loving and I love her dearly. I also called my mother and said "I'm going into the hospital; here's what the problem is," without being defensive, and say to her, "I really need you. Will you please come," and knowing that she would.

How do you feel about your work?

It means freedom. It's an arena for proving capability. It's an arena for saying in some subtle and not so subtle ways, You ain't gonna mess over me cause I am a competent professional, and so regardless of whether you have problems with the fact that I have a handicap or that I am a woman, you can go blow that out your ear, buster. This aggression is not quite as strong now as before, but I've laid that kind of number out loud and clear.

It's been the one place where it doesn't matter how I walk. I'm a good teacher, I'm a good consultant, I am learning to be a good university professor. Learning to be good at this new profession has nothing to do with my handicap, I just need to understand the new world of the university. When I do something that is competent, the handicap is unimportant. An article gets published, they don't know whether I'm handicapped or not. It's made me feel more competent, as opposed to that whole Christmas tree ornament kind of thing.

I'm trying to make work less important though because I think that there are some other things in life, like playing, and I'm learning to play. I didn't do it as a child, as a teenager, or a young adult. Even though there are limitations in terms of the kind of play that I can be involved in, like I can't run or play tennis, but I am finding that there are things that I can do and that I do enjoy. Like sailing—I can sail. And I can have a good time at it. And the fact that I'm scared to death of water I don't think is necessarily a function of having a handicap. I want to continue doing things like that, even have them be a larger part of my life than work.

Related to that, I think, are two beliefs I have that are the direct result of being handicapped and I feel really good about them. One is a desire to live. Well, it's more than a desire—a compulsion, an obsession to get the most out of life that I can. I find days and months and weeks to be very precious pieces of time; they're just too important to waste. The other is a learned sensitivity to other people, the sense of mortality that we all have as humans. I guess I'm feeling more a part of the human race now than I used to. But even when I felt that I was very separate from most normal people, I feel I developed a sensitivity over time, understanding constraints, understanding people's hopes and dreams, and their fears around not being able to achieve those hopes and dreams—that was something that was emphasized when I was growing up. And also being strong. I'm not sure I would be as strong as I am today if I hadn't been handicapped. That's something my father really almost beat into my head. However, I gave something up to be strong and that was not being vulnerable and soft. That's something I'm learning now, too, so it's like playing catch-up on one side.

Your profession is to teach administrators.

I train administrators to run special ed programs.

What is special education all about?

Special ed's a dumping ground for all the kids that nobody knows how to handle or wants to handle: the racist, sexist sub-system of education that mirrors our society. As we segregate in the larger society, we segregate in education. We teach kids that that's the way the world is and that it's important to sift out those who deviate, those who are different. And then the whole pupose of special ed is to try and get those kids to not be special, to emulate the norm as closely as possible so they can get back into regular kinds of programs with regular kinds of people. And we do a very bad job of it.

The whole premise is wrong. The premise should be that

everybody can learn something, that everybody has potential, that we need to look at the wide range of alternatives in terms of reaching kids—find out what they can learn, and that kids are important. They're real, they're human, and when we segregate them we deny their humanness. We think, "Well, maybe they're human, but not quite as much as these other third graders." I think all kids should be put back into regular education and we should have a system, an experimental arm of education, whose sole purpose would be to help teachers find ways of reaching the children in their classes. But that would be for a whole range of kids, not just the ones that we right now would call special ed kids.

We have some very gifted kids in certain areas. We need to nurture that. Teachers often don't know how to do that. We have some real exciting kids that we just tend to mold together, so everybody comes out in the twelfth grade as the same kind of product. And those who don't get molded along the way get beat and punished for not doing it.

What do you think of the argument that mainstreaming is going to put handicapped kids in a situation they can't handle?

Oh, I think that's true. Teachers are not prepared for it and neither are the kids. See, one of the things we've never really looked at is where is the kid at? We as adults certainly know so much more about them and we make the decision; we take a kid out of regular education and say, "Okay, now you're either a dummy or a cripple or a retard or crazy or something and we'll put you over here and then we're going to do some magic." One day the kid wakes up not realizing all that magic has been done and the teacher or whoever says, "Okay, even though you still are whoever we said you are, we're now going to allow you to go back into the regular ed class to try to do some things there; we're not sure you have the skills to do it, but we're gonna try." And we have not looked at what the kid needs, what the teacher needs, what the classroom needs.

Now I never put any kid that I taught in a regular education class until I worked with the teacher. Then I worked with the kids and we talked about what it means to be different and what it means to be pulled out of your own group and put someplace else. And I did the same talks with my people. I said, "Hey, you got a heavy number run on you and now you're going to have to go in there with that label and that's not going to be easy. But, here are some things maybe that we can do together to help you get ready." Certainly, some of them are academic; as presently constituted, you don't survive unless you can handle the assignments. But some are just social skills: you don't pick your nose, you don't talk out of turn, you raise your hand, you dress neatly, you know what's going on in school, and you have some sense of your environment. There is a norm, and if you are above that norm or below it, you are in big trouble.

Now I think that the purpose of education is to turn out workers, but not too many, because our society cannot have full employment. It is a sifting process, from kindergarten to the twelfth grade, and those kids that get left out are the nonworkers. Of those that graduate, some will go on and go through further sifting kinds of processes, and some will be sifted in terms of what's going on in the society. But we don't have to turn out the same kind of workers. We've got a factory right now. Cars move through stages on the assembly line at Ford, and kids do the same thing only we call them grades. And we fill kids' heads with an enormous amount of minutia and irrelevant information and lies, where we should be helping kids discover and learn how to find answers—that there's a wide range of alternatives, life is not A or B, good or bad, fat or skinny. I think one of the primary purposes of education should be to help people be independent, make their own decisions, to have skills to be part of the larger collective community.

I think education has been heavily related to the world of work. I don't think everybody has to work. I don't think everybody has to bust their ass every day. There are a wide variety of alternatives. You can work for six months and not work for six months. I would hope that this capitalistic society could change so that there would be degrees of work, so that working an hour a month wouldn't make me less of a person than somebody who works a hundred and sixty hours a month. That would put more emphasis on quality of life, and I'm not talking about material kinds of things. Everybody doesn't have to have two cars, and waste the way we do, but to have more caring, more interpersonal interaction, more acceptance of each other's differences. There can be sharing. And there are different kinds of work. It's like the rigid belief that kids only learn in school, that kids start to learn at age five, and they stop learning when they graduate, and everything that goes on outside of the school is not learning.

I don't think handicapped kids are ever expected to grow up and be independent. I don't think special ed fosters it, I don't think the community fosters it or society—and certainly parents of handicapped kids are members of that community and society. It's there, it's an assumption which is deeply embedded in our society: Handicapped people don't work, you give to charity, you have little sheltered workshops—and that's relatively new—but, mostly, they don't work.

We give them a whole lot of bullshit to learn. I learned how to weave hotpads, and I was supposed to learn how to sing so that I could enjoy myself at home, and reading was okay because that could be an activity that I could do while I was at home since it didn't take any physical exertion. We do not prepare children in special ed—handicapped children—to believe that they can be contributing, productive parts of the community. We maintain the myth. There are no handicapped people in textbooks that have made it, except for Roosevelt, who was not handicapped for a long time, and Helen Keller, one out of several million people. We have our standard "show cripples" as we've had our standard "show niggers." There isn't a pervading belief that all children can grow up to be productive, contributing adults.

What is the effect of that on the handicapped child?

Well, it depends on how that life gets played out. If you have no choices because you don't work, you are consigned to a room this size with a television set and that's it; you don't even have other people around. I think there's something exciting about being able to go outside, to be able to go to the show, to be able to buy a coke at the corner drugstore, to interact with other people. But when you don't work, in our society it's very difficult to interact with people, because one of the ways of interacting and building relationships with other people is through the world of work. You can't do it sitting in a room because your neighbors aren't going to come around. It's sentencing people to a very limited kind of life with no opportunity to fulfill themselves.

I can now work with others to assure at least access to the public schools for handicapped kids, and I am encouraged that the law is on our side. But I'm not encouraged because I know what kids are getting into in schools; whether or not they're handicapped, it's not really such a neat place to be. I was kind of encouraged when 504 was passed and then I was discouraged during the fight to get the regulations, and then when the regulations were passed, I was encouraged, and now I'm not so encouraged because the Office of Civil Rights is really not doing much. They're really dragging their feet. I think it's going to be a very long time before there's any kind of real impact. The agencies will fill out the appropriate forms, but there won't be a substantive kind of change and it will be selected people who are able to get into the whole mainstream of society. You know, just a real small issue, but it's also a very large one.

We've made little gains, but I don't think we're going to see a revolution, not like some of the professionals are talking about—the end of the quiet revolution. Maybe it's the end of the quiet one and the beginning of a loud one, but it's going to take an awfully long time to make the kinds of changes, and I'm not sure it's going to come about because I'm afraid of a backlash. Well, look at Proposition Thirteen in California where they cut the property tax. That is a backlash to governments' freely financing programs, so they're going to cut back. What does that mean in terms of education, and then what does it mean in terms of special ed? In order to make this thing work, this thing being 94-142 which includes IEPs and "least restrictive environment" and "due process" and so on, we're going to have to have a lot more people in the process. A lot more people costs a lot more money.

As long as we are saying that there shouldn't be abortions because that's a human life and that life deserves to live, and as long as we are saying that we do not believe in euthanasia because everybody has an opportunity to live, and as long as we are passing off as a belief that everybody can fulfill their potential, then we better put our money where our mouth is. I don't think that we really believe that. I mean, that's for some folks, but not for others. But I'm saying to society, I'm going to hold you to your word. You're saying that we're all entitled to a piece of the action. The courts have said that it does irreparable harm to withhold education from children. Well, as long as you're saying that, then you better start putting some money in and assuring handicapped children the access to the schools so that they can find their potential. And we need to redefine what potential is.

What do you think the place of disabled people is in our society?

I think we're expendable, we're an embarrassment, we're a fringe group. True, there are some of us who have made it as there have been blacks who have made it in America, and women, but by and large I think the whole issue of where handicapped people are at vis-à-vis society is everybody would be much happier if we stayed in institutions; undoubtedly they, because of a Judeo-Christian doctrine, would be willing to pay a certain amount of charity so that those people could live out their lives, but really they don't want to have a full integration of handicapped people into the mainstream of society.

Historically, I think there's lots of data for that view: handicapped children being sent to a different school, the number of institutions in this country for the mentally ill and mentally retarded, and within those institutions the number of physically handicapped people placed there, the development of segregated facilities for the blind and deaf in schools. The first group that really did anything with handicapped people was the Catholic Church. Nuns ran asylums. Before that, if you look at the history, you have the handicapped person as the court jester, as the beggar on the street, as victims of the witch hunts, which were very much in terms of women and, I think, handicapped women. There are some strong indications that a number of the witches burned were epileptics, or had some kind of physical deviation.

I think it's interesting that in this country we believe in the individual person—if you only work hard enough and do good and be white you can make it in our society. And so if you are mildly handicapped and if you don't make too big of a fuss, there is a place in the public schools for you. But if you begin to look at the whole national movement of deinstitutionalization for the mentally retarded and what communities went through in order to develop group homes with zoning boards and so forth, the same kind of arguments for not integrating the white community with blacks—the same kinds of arguments—were used for the handicapped. Would you want one living next door to you? They'll run down property values. Would you want one dating your daughter? They're all sex fiends. And there are lots of attitudes in this that I think are very analogous to the attitudes that surround other minority groups, and that get played out in the same way. The ghettos for the blacks are pest holes in cities; the ghettos for the mentally retarded are pest holes outside of the city, practically armed fortresses, but nobody's willing to see them or do anything about them.

I think our whole national position on the handicapped has been a charity kind of thing, a denial of respect, of humanness. Let us take care of you because you are incapable and incompetent to take care of yourself, and so we pass laws that sterilize handicapped women, and create myths about handicapped men. We deny handicapped people the opportunity to work, to play, to actively be involved in the life of the community. I am consistently appalled at the myths around whether or not handicapped people can relate to each other and normal people, whether they should be allowed to date, marry, have children, vote. I mean, it was just recently that they denied several women in a group home the opportunity to register to vote.

You look at churches. How in the hell is a person in a wheelchair going to get into most of the churches in any community? The whole flight of stairs. I mean, you can't even go to court. I went to the state building today so my daughter could take her road test. I called and asked if there was any handicapped parking. They said, "Oh, of course there is." I arrived to find a whole purple curb in back of the building for the handicapped to park. Fine. There's no curb cut! There is not a curb cut on all four sides of that building. Now the message to me is, Sure we'll let you drive, or get a license, or do any of the business that is required in this building—but you figure out how to get in. I don't think that our society wants us to be in.

The movie *Coming Home* is a story of a paraplegic Vietnam veteran. In San Francisco they were having a showing of that movie—and here it is, about a paraplegic—and it was in a theatre that wheelchairs could not get into. This is real indicative of what our society is like, the insensitivity to the needs of people who want to participate. It was kind of neat knowing that there was a demonstration, and they changed where the movie was going to be shown. But I'm not real encouraged. I think curb cuts are more for the bicyclist than for the handicapped person.

One reason for this exclusion is fear, fear of the unknown — I don't know what you're like and you act so much more differently than I do. That's scary. A fear of our own fragile sense of being. The whole issue of being whole, perfect — physically — is I think as important for men as women, although it works out differently. Women are supposed to have good figures, and nice long legs, a nice round ass, and big boobs, and that makes a good-looking woman. Well, what if you have 60 pounds of braces or one leg's shorter than the other? How do men become men? They participate in physical activity. They jump out of the car and open the door for a woman. They do physical kinds of things and when that's not there, what are you left with?

After World War I when vocational rehabilitation came in it was because our country had to do something for able-bodied men who came back and were no longer able-bodied. They could not say, "You are worthless," because they fought in a war, an American kind of activity. And so out of a sense of responsibility, they did certain kinds of things. I think the Second World War should show the same kinds of things, although if you look at the Vietnam war, they aren't providing those kinds of services to those men. We only want a few show cripples in this country and that's about it. Very limited access.

I think basically these human services are part of a delivery system which is based upon the premise that the client, the patient, the recipient is incapable of handling their own affairs, and the process dehumanizes you whether you're talking about welfare or vocational rehabilitation or special ed. We created dependency upon the human care system and the whole purpose is not to make people independent because if they got independent then those people who are delivering the services would no longer be useful and we can't afford that. So we create mammoth institutions for providing services that in the long run don't do very much.

We have a whole system we call charity as well as quasi-charitable organizations such as sheltered workshops. How many vocational rehabilitation counselors do you know that are handicapped? Most of the goddamn buildings you can't get into. So we have the able-bodied taking care of the handicapped. Those who are sound in mind and spirit and soul and body. Who has ever said to the handicapped, What do you want? What would make you independent? What kinds of things need to occur so that you can be part of this life and have a mutual exchange?

I can only talk for me, I can't talk for all handicapped people because we're not homogeneous. We're a heterogeneous aggregate of individuals that's been lumped together as a group. I am not blind, so I cannot say for even one other blind person what their needs are. Generally speaking, I want to be provided a chance to participate in community life, to be educated, to be part of religion if that's what I choose to do, to be able to move about the city, to be able to live in decent housing where I choose to live, to be able to select jobs that are meaningful, to flow, and to listen to each other. I think we could come up with very creative solutions to present day problems, creative ways of relating to each other, creative ways of improving the quality of life.

If you bring together different nationalities or different cultures there is a growing and sharing that can take place that you don't get when you have everybody thinking alike. There isn't the discovery, there isn't the learning that takes place. From taking handicapped children and putting them into regular classrooms, able-bodied children can learn different realities: what it's like to function from a wheelchair as opposed to standing up straight. They can gain insights into a person that is raised differently, that has different experiences. One of the things that scares me is that we don't give our children the skills to handle themselves if they're not able-bodied. At some point most all of us are not going to be able-bodied, at least for a short period, and to be able to gain those kinds of skills, I think is important for being able to move on.

You were talking about charity beforehand in a very derogatory way. What does charity mean to you?

At a macro level it means I'll give you a few bucks and you'll stay out of my life; I don't want to follow up where those bucks go or whatever, but if we have a cute little cripple kid on a poster, I'll give a few bucks and that will take care of my responsibilities.

At a micro interpersonal level it puts the person receiving the charity in a one-down position. You are beholden to the person who is giving out the goodies. In order to receive, say, funds for medical care, you're stripped of all dignity to get it. And you're to feel guilty for asking for it. I think the whole social services business is just like that. If you are a charity patient in a hospital, you're treated differently, because it's like you're not doing what you should be doing; the person who receives it is looked upon as someone who is less human. Now that's where Aid to Dependent Children, or Aid to the Disabled, or the Lion's Club are. There are degrees, I wouldn't paint every aspect of charity with the same strokes. But, generally speaking, it requires that the handicapped person be dependent and that the person who is giving the charity is better than the person receiving it. And so one is up and one is down.

Oh yes, I've made it and yes I am middle class and I've got some bucks, and I can say that in a philosophical kind of way. But as a child, I was the recipient of the so-called charity and I think it sucks. Charity gives out lots of bad messages, but I also think that the whole care giving institution, whether it's charity or whatever, has the same intrinsic dependency built into it, and I'm opposed to it.

It can't be done away with, not as our society's presently constituted. We cannot eliminate the charitable aspect because too many people will be hurt and could die or just be relegated to a never-never land. But there are differing forms of charity. If the Christian definition of charity was really played out, I'm not opposed to that kind. But I'm talking about the kind of charity that really exists and how its operationalized.

So what do you do about it?

I'd like to do away with charity, as well as with the whole volunteer movement; but I also know that if you do away with either one or both, you lose an incredible amount of resources that would not otherwise be there because our society is not organized to fill in the gap. I think one of the little, tiny glimmers of hope is education. If it can change so that kids can develop and believe that they're okay, then the charity process will not be debilitating to them.

Oh, on one hand, I know it has to be done, otherwise there'll never be the funds to do the kinds of things that are required. And on the other hand I am appalled at the whole process. You don't pick out little kids, or big people, or anyone and show them up and say feel sorry for them so we can get money. I hate that aspect—feel sorry for them, pity them, scare folks. Oh God, it could happen to me. But you look at the March of Dimes, that's exactly what they did. And they were able to do some phenomenally good things. And, certainly I don't think that polio would have been eradicated without it. Some people would not have lived without it. But the way in which it had to be done I am still opposed to, although I would never do anything to eliminate that kind of group, based on our present structure. It's a real Catch 22.

The way I see the big picture and the way I see things professionally is intimately tied up with who I am, and how I feel, and I feel that as a person with a handicap I've gotten ripped off. People have done their level best to assure that I won't make it. All of that, combined with a good feeling about who I am, then contributes to what I see as the big picture and how I operate professionally. I'm torn between what I see really, really wrong with education—and part of what I see is wrong with education is what happened to me in my own personal history—and what are the good things that have happened in terms of education and good parts of my personal history. So there's always that dichotomy. My dislike of charity is directly tied into the "feel sorry for" kinds of experiences that I had as a child.

I won't bomb the March of Dimes office, but I will make impassioned speeches about how charity is a dehumanizing process. I would much prefer that people receive what they need in terms of resources, but that they don't pay with their dignity and their humanity. Now you're getting into that little part of me that I keep hidden usually, the idealistic one. The one who wants the utopia.

Liza DiMaggio

Liza is a perky child growing into a vibrant adolescent. She is bright, sensitive, articulate, and opinionated. Her insight is one side of her story. The experience informing her understanding is the other side.

Sometimes it seems hard to reconcile Liza's words with her youth. It is not because she is brave, nor because she is smart — it is because she is grown up before her time. The worlds of hospitals, of stigma, and of self-consciousness are worlds usually reserved for adults. Liza's disability catapulted her into that world before adulthood. She is wise about those worlds because she knows them. That such wisdom is possible in certain parts of Liza's worlds might lead us to believe that access to similar sorts of wisdom are available to all of us. And, we might reckon, Liza's education and development have profited by learning from her experience and using that learning to develop other wisdom, knowledge and reason.

It is hard to avoid the impression that Liza has many strengths which an able-bodied person her age might not have and that these strengths if encouraged could illuminate her education and her life. If so, it is a lesson to the educator that there are strengths in handicapped children and these strengths can be built upon in a truly "special" education. Building from strength is a prudent policy not only in education, but in the multitude of other relationships which constitute our society.

I have transverse myelitis. It's a viral infection of the spinal cord. It started with a cold last November, when I was twelve. I

70

had bronchitis, which I often get in the winters anyway, and then I went into tracheitis, and I was in the hospital for two weeks and I was in an oxygen tent on the ultrasonic mist. They have this thing called the bird, it's a respirator for inhalation therapy, and I would go into coughing spasms for about six hours at a time without stopping.

A few days before I was supposed to go home, I started vomiting all over the place and having diarrhea. They thought that it was just intestinal virus, so they sent me home two days late. I went home the day before Thanksgiving and I dehydrated, I couldn't keep anything down. My mother called the doctor and told him I was dehydrating. She's an RN, and she is still going to school for a B.S. degree, and he said, "Oh! Once you women go to school and learn a little bit you get so panicky." She's been going to school for four years to know a little bit, you know what I mean? He has some nerve. My mother has spent a lot of money and time going to school when she's got two kids at home that she's got to take care of and they are just at the point where they need a lot of parental guidance—and he says that she knows a little bit. I have a lot of respect for my mother. I know how hard she has worked.

Anyway, she told the doctor, I'm bringing her in in an hour and you better be there. Then she tried to work me up in fluid. Like she's give me one tablespoon, and then she'd give me two tablespoons, and she worked it up to three ounces and I started vomiting again. So she gave me a tablespoon and I just vomited. I was dehydrating very badly, hearing high-pitched noises and muffled sounds, and I was hallucinating. Then my pulse rate was very low, and my blood pressure was low, and my mother and my older brother brought me in to the hospital. When I got there, the doctor said I was dehydrated, and that he was glad she did bring me in. He said that by the next day I would have been in a coma.

So they put me on an IV and I was conscious, but I didn't know who was in the room. I knew that something was happening, but I didn't know what, and I didn't care. After three weeks of IV therapy and not being able to eat a single thing or drink anything, I started getting better and I went home. Then I started having diarrhea again five or six times a day, and sometimes seven. They had been giving me drugs in the hospital,

tranquilizers and things to settle your stomach. I just started having abdominal distention and cramps and gas pockets. Like a whole bubble would be standing up on my stomach. My mother didn't know what it was, so she took me to the doctor. That was when I started really bad cramps. The vomiting had stopped by that time, but the diarrhea was getting worse. I went back to him and he took X-rays, and he said maybe it was an intestinal blockage because there was a lot of gas and the diarrhea was seepage. So they put me on twelve ounces of mineral oil a day in three sections. First they tried eight ounces and that didn't do anything, so they tried twelve ounces and I just kept on having diarrhea. Then I started vomiting oil because it was irritating my stomach. It really got bad and I started dehydrating again. Also, about this time, I started being incontinent of my urine. Like I would never know when it would come and never feel it or anything.

Then I was transferred to another, supposedly better, hospital because they thought I was weak and having loss of balance. They had me on all sorts of medication for pain because my stomach was getting really bad. At the hospital they said it was all in my mind, that I was pampered and spoiled and I was trying to get attention, that I was making myself vomit, it was all psychosomatic, and my parents should take me home. They did do an upper GI series and a barium enema, but all they found was an irritated ileum, part of the intestines, and they did it so badly that they had to do it again, which irritated my doctor very much. If they had taken the neurological exam or lumbar puncture, you know, the spinal tap, at the first sign of myelitis, the incontinence of the urine, they would have found out right away and I wouldn't be in this stupid wheelchair.

As it was they didn't even take many tests. The hospital was so psycho-oriented that it's unbelievable. They used to tell the girl in traction next to me that her pain was not there, that she was simply imagining it. As for me, I had been running a temperature for three months, and then all of a sudden it started going higher. It was just a low grade temperature for three months and they ignored it completely. Telling me it's all in my mind. How can you ignore a low grade temperature for three months?

So then I went to another hospital. They had to repeat the

GI series because it had been done so bad in that other hospital. In the new hospital, I was in isolation for a long time because they were doing all kinds of tests. They thought I might have Hodgkin's disease, cancer, rheumatic fever, or TB. They thought I had TB because I had been exposed to active TB from my neighbor upstairs. So they took all sorts of tests. Some were positive and some were negative, and all sorts of stupid things.

But my present doctor says if they'd just given me a spinal tap, I wouldn't be in this chair. A few weeks ago I would not even have been able to sit in this chair; I would be leaning like this because I just couldn't hold myself up. Now I still have to hold on a little bit, but when I have my legs out in front of me I can sit up pretty good.

How did you react to all of this testing and speculation?

I was always aggressive, active and independent. Now I'm starting to get a lot more independent again. But for a while there, when I was still in bed and I was on IVs, thinking I had cancer, I had given up. I almost died a couple of times of dehydration. I was on seven injections of codeine and other narcotics a day for pain because it was so intense. I couldn't drink or eat anything. After a while they thought it might have been that I was scared, but they couldn't find any reason for the vomiting because it was caused by the spinal cord—the wrong impulses and stuff. They treated me a lot better, they did. And they found that the liver and spleen were both enlarged quite a bit.

How do you like the hospital you are in now?

In most ways this is about the best hospital I've ever been in. The food is pretty good. And the recreation is good here, too. I like this place, but I still would rather be home.

I want to be with my parents, I love my parents very much. I want to be with my friends, I want to go to school, I want to learn. Let's face it, it's a good school here, but not as good as at home. You've got to admit that. You really do. My friend, who was here for two years for asthma, said that when it came time to go home her family had moved twice since she had been here, and she didn't know anybody at home, and she didn't even want to go home. She had become so used to the place that it was home. She would like to see her parents more and her family more, but she was afraid to go home because she didn't know what it was going to be like. She didn't know anybody. She hadn't been to school at home in two years and she was afraid. I can understand that. And I think that when it comes time for me to go home, I'm going to be afraid, too.

It's going to be hard to adjust, I know that. It was hard to adjust to being very sick, but it wasn't that hard. You sort of lead up to a place like this, you know, slowly. But all of a sudden you're gonna go home and go right back to school, and it is not like you can adjust like that.

I would go home now if I could, but only if I were walking, because it depresses my family a lot, I know. Sometimes it gets my mother upset that I don't do things that she would like me to do, but yet she doesn't want me to do them because she's afraid I might get hurt and she feels bad about that, too.

There's a lot of things I'm not sure of — about walking, about my parents, about my friends. Sometimes I feel that when I go home my friends do treat me differently. Like they talk to me differently sometimes, or are nicer, although my best friend doesn't do that.

I do like to be with people, and here in the hospital I play with kids and I go outside on the green unit with the smaller kids. I play with them a lot. The babies here need a lot of love. They are much more mature than most kids their age. They don't cry and scream like kids do at home. They are not whiney little kids. I think that they are better behaved than other kids are, but I think they need a lot more love than other kids do.

A lot of them are a lot more intelligent than other kids. Like there's this little kid, Alex, that's here. I think he has CP, I'm not sure. But he has such a wide vocabulary, and he's only three years old. He's a nasty little thing, but he's very intelligent. He's so cute, he's really adorable. When I go up to another kid, Larry, I say, "What you got there, Larry?" He'll say, "Don't you take that away from me. The nurse can't have it." I say "Don't worry, I'm not a nurse and I'm not going to take it." Then he says, "OK, you can play with it." They are really good kids.

Would you like to work with kids?

I want to be a doctor, I'm not sure what kind. I think I'd like to be a pediatrician or neurologist or something like that. I want to work with little kids a lot because I love babies. Or maybe I'll be just a plain pediatrician, maybe specializing in CP or muscular dystrophy or just general rehabilitation. I would like to work in a place like this. However, I don't want to be a nurse, because they generally don't have that much to do, you know what I mean?

I've always loved to play with little kids. My neighbors have a retarded child for a foster child. I play with her a lot. Lots of kids ask me how I could have the patience to play with her, and I tell them that she's no different than I am except maybe in her personality and mentality, and that doesn't mean I can't love her. It doesn't mean I can't try to help her, or be towards her as I would want somebody to be towards me. I play with her, and I try to make games that she would enjoy because she doesn't like to exercise. So I sort of take exercises and make it into a game like Simon Says. Like doing kneebends and running around playing tag and stuff. She likes it, and that's the whole thing.

How do you see yourself now?

Before I was handicapped, I always had a lot of respect for people with handicaps. I always was very interested, very curious. It's my nature to be nosy, and I always wanted to know more about people. When I saw a person in a wheelchair, I would just go up and tell them that I'm curious, and ask whether they had CP or muscular dystrophy, or were paraplegic or something. I wouldn't make it obvious but I would let them know that I would like to know, not because I'm a snotty kid but because I really care.

Now I see that it can be very embarrassing to go up and ask a person if they have CP, or why they are in a wheelchair. Like if you don't put it so bluntly, it might be a little better. Sometimes a kid will stare at me and I know that they don't mean it or anything, but it makes me feel bad because I know that a year ago I could climb a tree, I could run, I could swim, and I could be just like them, and it hurts. I mean I've always been very active, I was on the swimming team, or I used to be anyway, since I was seven years old. I learned to swim the dog paddle when I was two, and I learned to do the regular swimming when I was five. I have twenty ribbons for swimming; four second prizes, two third, the rest first. I'm proud of that. It upsets me sometimes to see myself this way, because it's just not the same as I was a year ago.

A lot of times I'm sitting in Physical Therapy right in front of the big wall mirror, and I'll be looking at myself, and I'll be saying to myself, That's not you, you know. What do you look like when you're standing up by yourself, or when you're in a pool, or when you're running and playing with your puppy? What do you look like just walking to school, or just being yourself in the trees like last year? How do your parents feel about this? Why? Just why? I ask myself that a lot. Sometimes it gets very depressing because there is no answer for it. There is no reason. Sometimes I get downright obnoxious for no reason, sometimes I just get moody.

Since I have been in a wheelchair I have noticed a lot of other things about myself. Like that I move a lot, without even knowing it. A lot of times I'll be sitting at the dinner table, and I'll just be going like this and I won't even realize it. I have always been, you might say, hyperactive. Not that I look for trouble or that I'm a trouble-maker or anything. I can't help it, I can't stay still, especially since I've been in that cribby over there. That machine stinks, I'd like to kick it. I'd like to burn it. I don't know why I hate my wheelchair. I honestly don't know. It's a mechanical device that is doing for me something that I want to be doing myself. It's sort of like a setback. You know what I mean. It's like keeping me from doing a lot of things that I would like to do. And it annoys me very much.

Sometimes I feel, I don't know, sometimes I feel scared. Sometimes I feel that my therapist pushes me too hard, that she wants something I can't deliver. And sometimes I feel that she thinks that I just don't want to give my all. But I do. It's not that I don't want to, it's just that I can't deliver as fast or as good as she'd like me to. And there are times when she's telling me I can, I can, and I'm telling her I can't, I can't, I can't. And even though I'm telling myself I can, I can, I can, and I'm trying, a lot of times it just doesn't happen. And that gets very depressing, too.

I just get depressed that I can't see myself as I was, that I can't even remember what I looked like. A lot of times I used to climb trees. We have a swing in the backyard that my brother and I made with a rod, and cable. We used to just hang on it and swing. My brother made it lower for me at home. He said "Shall I fix it for you?" Like I almost wanted to cry, you know what I mean? My brother has been very neglected since I have been sick.

He has been treated more like he was an adult and has been deprived of his feelings. So it makes me feel both good and sad that my brother would do something like that just to make me happy.

Other things have changed, too. Last weekend I felt bad because my mother wouldn't let me go by myself to my friends's house, and she just lives on the next block. I got very upset, yelling and screaming. I even cried about it, I was saying, "Why do you treat me different now? You say you would like to see me as independent as I was before, but yet won't let me be. You let me do more things that a lot of my handicapped friends' parents let them do, but yet you don't let me do my full capacity. You keep me from doing things that are very important to me, like going to my friend's house, and like it's important for me to be able to do things for myself and be out as much as I was before."

Maybe I am hiding the reality from myself, but I just don't want to be treated different. I want to be me. I don't want to be treated as the me that's now in the wheelchair, the handicapped me, the sick me. I want to be treated as myself. I'm not sick anymore. I'm not dehydrating. I've gained back my weight. That's how I want to be treated. I want to be treated as my friends are treated, I want to be treated as a healthy kid, not as a sick or handicapped kid. Because I'm not. I think handicap is in your mind. That's the only way you can be handicapped, because if you are going to tell yourself that you're handicapped and that you can't do this and you can't do that, then naturally you're not going to be able to do it. Because you don't believe you can, you don't want to really.

I mean, suppose I say I can't swim because I don't have my legs. I can swim. I've been in the pool and I can swim just as well as before, maybe not as fast but that doesn't mean anything. Suppose I say I can't communicate with other people because I am in a wheelchair and they wouldn't understand. That's a cop-out. Another cop-out is saying that I cannot do as well as you can at your business because I'm handicapped, or I cannot do up to my full capacity because I am handicapped. That's a cop-out. That's what I feel is in your mind. Take my friend who cannot write with her hand. She has joint disease, but she can write with her mouth. She can still write and that's what counts. It is because she tries and that's what counts. And I try a lot but sometimes I feel that I'm not trying, and sometimes I don't know why but sometimes I just don't feel like trying. Sometimes, I just get so depressed I don't want to think about it. Like sometimes I don't care anymore, sometimes I feel like I don't care, but I really do.

There is a sixty to seventy percent chance of completely recovering. They did an electromylogram that said they should hope that there would be no permanent nerve damage. But if there is damage I might be using braces and crutches. But I'm not going to stop here. I am going to work until I am satisfied that I can't go any further.

I don't want to think about not walking. I think I'm afraid to. I always wanted to be in the Olympics for swimming, but now I feel that it's not that important any more. I'd rather be a doctor and help people than get a medal for swimming, and it has always been a big part of my life. So has school, and making people happy. I'm good at art, and with kids.

Do people relate to you differently now than before your illness?

I kind of think it makes people feel bad to see me in a wheelchair. It's not that I care that they feel that I can't walk or that I'm crippled—to use a word that I hate. It annoys me the way people use it. They use it to torment. Not all the time. Not all people do, but some do, and it hurts. I've seen it happen to friends that I care about, and that makes me very angry.

I went to a restaurant about three weeks ago with my parents that I had gone to before I was sick and I found it hard to cope with it cause when we were playing the jukebox, my brother and I, all the people would keep coming up and giving us quarters. After a while you begin to feel bad, like, here I am having people give me all this money to play on the jukebox whereas they wouldn't have done it a year ago, but it also makes you feel good in a way that people care. But they can only show their feelings in a certain way.

I think that if people really want to show their feelings they will do things for the handicapped that matter, not a lousy quarter to play a lousy two songs on the jukebox. Like, take the same restaurant, for instance, I couldn't get into the bathroom. And if I could get in the door I couldn't get in the little wells that they have for you to go because they're so narrow. And if I were alone in that restaurant, there would be absolutely no way that I could get into it. Somebody might have helped me, but that would be quite embarrassing.

Handicapped people sometimes have a lot more wisdom than other people because they can know about people's feelings and really care. They know that they have gone through a lot of suffering, too, that they have really had to grow up a lot faster and mature a little more than other people so that they could really survive. I think that handicapped people don't generally feel sorry for themselves and don't expect other people, when they're sick or have a problem, to feel sorry for themselves either.

What other ways could people show they care?

People should make provisions for handicapped people, such as putting ramps on buildings. How many times I have gone to a place that I can't even get into without having to crawl up the stairs on my behind. I have to pull myself up on my ass, and rip my pants just so I can get into a lousy restaurant. My father would break his neck trying to get me up there in the stupid wheelchair because the steps are not wide enough. They could make half of the steps a ramp. I've gone into a department store in the new mall. It was just finished a couple of months ago, and they don't have a ramp. They don't have an elevator, and the elevators that they do have are for bringing mannequins upstairs. They're filthy, greasy, stinky and dirty. And I have to go in that to get upstairs, just to get a lousy dress. All because they can't even make provisions for a person in a wheelchair, or who has crutches, or a cane, or a walker.

People don't think. The majority aren't handicapped, and so they don't think about those things when they are building. And they should. I think that people care, but they should take time to really sort out the problems of people, to make provisions for all people, not just for one type of person. If you count all the handicapped people in this world you'll find out that a lot of people are in wheelchairs or have canes, or walkers. If people really cared as much as they say they do, then they would do these things, they would make these provisions, not just say "Yeah, yeah, yeah," and then forget about it.

They need to take time out from making a living all the time and think about other people's needs, not just their own. If people weren't so busy trying to make a living maybe they would understand what we people are trying to say, what we kids and young people are trying to say. They might find that it's very important.

I'm trying to say that people just can't always be thinking about themselves, they can't always be saying, "Well, all these steps are going to be so pretty, and this escalator is so handy for us not to have to push buttons and wait for the elevator." If more people would just take time out from making a living and always thinking of money and how to make living easier for themselves, then maybe they would be able to fulfill other people's needs, too. People just don't think about these things.

We are people, also. We are intelligent beings, even if we can't talk or communicate as well as or have as good coordination as people in general do. I think that I would want them to know that we care about them and that they should care about us too. We love just like they love. Thirteen-year-old handicapped kids have boyfriends just like thirteen-year-old nonhandicapped kids do. Don't they think that we love people, too, that we would like to have nice things, too, that we would like to go on a shopping spree some day, too, or go in Sears and go up the stairs and down the stairs and have some hamburgers with our friends? They make some of these stores so small that you can't even get in them. And that's not fair. I couldn't even get into this place to try on a pretty dress that I wanted to get and a halter and a pair of pants. I couldn't even get into the goddamn place to try it on, and I couldn't go into another place because they wouldn't let me into another store to try it on, so I couldn't get it. And if they would let me take it home and try it on, then they wouldn't let me take it back if it didn't fit.

And I think that the schools are very inconsiderate, too, because they have to make special schools just for people with handicaps. I don't think that I would like to go to a special school. I want to be with all kinds of people. If they would have a lousy elevator in the school, it would help. They have a tiny little elevator, three feet high, for projectors and TVs. They could take that apart and put in a new one. They could have a regular elevator and use it for equipment and for anybody who was in a wheelchair, too. There's a boy in my school who has CP. He used to walk with crutches and now he walks with a cane. It's very hard for him to go upstairs, and sometimes it even makes him late because we have three floors.

I just feel that I would like people to know how I feel and how other people feel and how inconsiderate people are sometimes without realizing it. They have to stop and think for a minute. Then they would see how mixed up this whole nation is, that there's provisions for certain people and no provisions for other people. There's not only handicapped people in a wheelchair, there's also handicapped people that can't see, and can't hear. Maybe people can get up the stairs, but maybe they can't get down the stairs if they can't see where they are going. A lot of times people ignore people that are deaf, and they find it hard to communicate, because people who are deaf can speak but not very well. It's hard to understand them, but if you stop and try you can. I know sign language. My sister's a special education teacher. She teaches the deaf and blind, and she teaches sign language. I have a neighbor who lives down the street from me who is deaf, and I talk to her all the time. She reads lips very well. She speaks with sign language and she also speaks, though not very well. But if I take time out I can understand her. And I think other people should try to, also. The more you ignore people, the more ignorant you become. I don't think people really understand, you know. All kinds of people are handicapped, no matter whether they are black, white, red, yellow, even if they are purple with polka-dots, people still have handicaps. People are still people. And they should be treated like people. I thought human rights was supposed to mean more than property rights, but sometimes I don't think they do. I really think that people should take time out to make this place a better world to live in.

We have people right here in this very country and this very state that are starving to death. People are starving to death living in rat-infested holes. Did you hear about the woman whose eight-year-old son was killed in an abandoned building next door to her? The welfare wouldn't even give her enough money to give him a decent burial and decent clothes for her kids to go to his funeral in. And that lady looked like she was sixty-five years old and she was thirty-two. Now I think that is disgusting. If people can't even care about people who are starving to death in this country, how can they care about handicapped people? That's why I say that we have a big problem to solve here. And the ones who have to solve it are the young people and us kids.

I listen to Dick Gregory records a lot, and I find him very interesting, and I find that a lot of what he has to say is true. I think that we young people and kids have a pretty big job to do in this nation to clean up this world, to clean up our government. You see how it's falling apart now. I think that generations ago the people turned this nation upside down and now we have to right it, and we can't unless people let our minds be free first. Grown-ups and older people are so busy destroying kids' lives that they don't let us live. They program us, they don't let us have our own imaginations because they stick it with what we *should* know, or what they think we should know. They begin lying to us from the age of two years old about Santa Claus. The first letter a kid writes is to somebody who doesn't exist.

We have to right this world, and it's been upside down for a long time. Not that our parents didn't try or anything. Changing the system isn't the easiest thing to do, but still you can start by making provisions like a ramp and a lousy elevator in a stupid building. You have to start with human rights, not property rights. Once people start making provisions for all people and not just the majority, then this world will start to right itself. I think that the only way the situation will change will be by people stopping, thinking, and caring, and really wanting to do something about it. I know I want to, and I know I want to help kids, I want to help people, that's why I want to be a doctor.

And I think that that's about all I have to say: That I like this hospital; I think it's very good. I hope I'll walk again, I like the kids here, and I have a lot of fun, but I would still rather be home.

Two Children

Handicapped children are those handicapped people we are most likely to encounter, particularly through the media. The situation of the disabled child is frequently tragic and society's construction of that situation only makes it more tragic. Frequently the childhood of the handicapped person is attributed to him by society long after childhood has passed.

The disabled children I talked to were in a hospital and a school reserved for the handicapped. Many of their questions, unlike many of the adults who speak in these pages, are unresolved. If the adults have made it, making it is a very real question for the children. If they do not make it, and many will not, it is predominantly because of the structure of social oppression, degradation, isolation, desexualization, and so on. What to do about these? One easy answer is a wholesale change in attitude. Unfortunately, and without a reason, such change in attitude rarely comes. One reason for that change will be an alliance of handicapped children with their parents, with disabled people, and professionals. It will require remarkable organization which, however, is already underway.

Thomas Brewster

"Second Wind"

When the big leaves and small leaves
End up on the ground
Small children walk without a sound

84

The tall children and small children
Jump onto the ground
Then they pick up all the leaves they see around
Finally a big pile is towering on the ground
Then they jump in and all leaves leave the ground
Without a sound

I'm twelve years old now. When I was born I had stuff on my arteries in my head. As I grew up it began to grow into a bag, and now it presses on some of my nerves so that my hands shake and stuff and I can't walk. I lost my center of gravity.

I first noticed it when I was about eight and a half. I went to get something out of the refrigerator, a pan or something, and hand began to shake. As I went to put it down, it shook so that some of the stuff in the pan spilled out and I got very, very scared. I told my mother and she said, "Don't worry, it's just nerves." I told her I thought we better go to the doctor and she said no, it's probably just nerves. So I went a couple more days, and then it got worse and my right hand was beginning to shake, then both hands. The whole left side was affected, even my eye, they just all winked, my whole left side all the time. My mother finally decided that we'd go to the doctor about two months after that time. We went to the doctor and the doctor said, "He's got a tumor and he'll have to be put in the hospital." So, I got put in the hospital when I was about nine. And then everything happened, the surgery and things.

I'm going to a hospital in Sweden where they have a new kind of cobalt treatment that's supposed to work. Without it, I might die, I don't know. I almost died once because of spinal fluid backing up, giving me too much pressure in my head. I would have died if the doctor hadn't saved me.

How are you able to talk about that stuff without becoming very, very emotional?

I've learned to control it for some reason. I don't know, I just learned that I had to accept it somewhat. I was told once that I should let everything all out, how I feel about things. Sure I'm scared. They told me once before that I was going to have an angiogram. An angiogram is when they stick a long needle (you have to be awake for it) down through your leg, all the way to the arteries, and then they have some sort of TV that shows it and they stick wires up in there for some reason. I had something very much like an angiogram — a radiogram, I think — a long time ago, and that was very hectic. The medicine that they gave me made me get very violent, and in the operating room I pushed the doctors out of the way and the thing wasn't successful. They had to weave a wire, I think all the way up to the tumor, and shoot pellets. Two of the pellets missed and they just went right through my system.

I guess the biggest things in your life right now are the medical things, but what about your feelings about your family, or about school?

Well, I have one brother, one sister, and a mother and a father. My father works too much because of the doctor bills and the insurance. We had about fifteen thousand dollars and that began to run low, so that's why he's working so hard. And, my father does all the work in our house, all alone, and has practically rebuilt the house by making new floorings, tearing down walls, rebuilding, putting up wallpaper, putting in electrical wiring and new pipe all by himself. He's done the living room, put down red carpet and everything, and the dining room, tearing up the whole floor and taking the walls down, and it looks beautiful now.

I feel really bad because they're really working so hard for me. My father works in a company — he fixes company machines and he sells them. My medical bills have been hard on my family. I feel rather confused about that. I feel like I would like to participate and earn money for my parents. It's like I'd like to pay them all back but I can't. I guess I have to live with it.

Do you get along with your brother and sister?

Yeah, I do — very well. My brother is fifteen now. My sister I think is sixteen. Sometimes I know I get too grouchy and I snap at everybody when I'm not supposed to. Sometimes I get aggravated, and I accidentally throw out all my anger on my sister and brother. They've done that quite a lot to me, too. They're not jealous, or anything like that. Oh, when I would be in my bed at home, they used to resent that. But now it's ok. Really, I resent them cause they get around more. I missed the family reunion with cousins who came a long way, and that's really rotten.

Were you in the wheelchair when you were in school?
No. But my hands were shaking then. Everybody used to make jokes about them. I got very mad at what they said. I'd like to say to them, "Did anybody know that you were very, very stupid about what you said a long time back? Just wait until you have a medical problem, and then seen what you have to say." One of the kids who was teasing me, the one that was bothering me the most, had a heart attack, a heart problem. I don't think he'll ever bother me again.

Would you rather go to a special school, like this place, or a regular school?
Some school like this with only handicapped kids, until I'm well, that is. Nobody here can tease me cause they've all got problems too. I guess it's o.k. If anybody's waiting for anything it's a hard place to be.

I understand you're into writing and photography. Tell me about the kind of stuff you've been writing.
Poetry, and books. I don't know. I like a lot of stories. I just feel like doin' 'em. I got about five different booklets of poetry by Whitman. Most of the poetry I've written is when I was sick in bed and it's what I really wanted to do, and right now I've been working on two books. One's about a dog who's going to die pretty soon and I want to finish it before he dies because he's a nice dog. One good thing is I've got typewriters to use, electric. I can only write a little. Otherwise my hand gets too pained and it starts hurting and I can't write, it doesn't want to work.

I'll tell you a poem. I remember one of my first ones. It's called "The Cat and the Rat."

> There once was a cat that had no purr.
> There once was a rat that had no fur.
> But one day this rat had a great spat,
> With a dear old cat and a big old cat,
> It ended so politely as you see,
> The big cat in a basket,
> the big rat in a casket.

That's the first one I ever did. I have lots of things, all typed up and put into a portfolio.

What do you think about the future, your future?

I hope that it will be ok. I don't know if it will or not, it might not. It might be rather difficult. I might not be the same person, but I know I want to be a photographer and a writer.

I guess I wanted to be a photographer when I began to get sick. A long time ago I had a small, cheap box camera, and I had been taking pictures and they turned out so beautiful. Not color, but black and white, for a show—they said they had to be black and white prints, beautiful, full album and everything and maybe you might win an electric eye Minolta camera. And I thought, I must, I've gotta do this if I want to be a photographer. And then before I could finish I got thrown in the hospital.

My mother is bringing me a box camera cause she accidentally threw out my old one. I have a polaroid camera, but the film costs about five dollars a pack. Box camera film costs about one dollar and that way I can take more pictures.

What do you take pictures of?

I take pictures up here of handicapped kids, color pictures of handicapped kids who I have known for awhile. Like, there are Perthes—maybe you don't know what they are, but they are like kids who are in braces because their hips are out of joint—there are kids in casts, the asthmatics. I'm thinking about writing something about handicapped kids and I've got all the names put down with the pictures. I'll write about the Perthes—the rough life they go through, the asthmatics—the very, very difficult life they go through. There's a kid in a wheelchair here who fell out of a seven-story window, and he cannot talk, he can hardly see, and he's a very mixed up boy. He can walk, except he bumps into things and he immediately falls. The skull is completely gone on one whole side of his head, it's only skin, so his brain is right out in the open. I want to take pictures of all these kids and write about what happened and, I don't know, write about how it could have happened—better ways to make sure that people won't be accidentally handicapped like that. I feel like calling it *The Handicapped World.*

What kind of world is the handicapped world?

Well, people are in braces, people are in casts, people are in wheelchairs and stretchers, in lifemobiles like the Perthes. People have to do exercises in physical therapy, go to special schools. Everybody's life is rough.

I'd like to find out if all the asthmatics' lives are roughly the same, or if the problems are more difficult at certain ages. Like, you see, young kids, they might not think about how rough their life is, but older kids, they really will think about it. So I want to see if the older ones or the younger ones are worse off. Because asthma, when you're young, builds up and there's more mucus in your body than when you're older because your chest expands, and there's just a small pool of mucus down there. But, the young kids are all congested and everything, they're all full of mucus and when they have attacks, they're in a lot of trouble. Asthmatics could die, like if you spray deodorant in their room to freshen it. They feel very scared about something in there. They'll run right out and not come back until they are certain that someone has gone into that room and cleared it.

And most kids are probably like that. A lot of kids have to go through braces, a lot of people, even nurses. There's a nurse in the old hospital I was at and when she was working as a nurse in the Army the army base was attacked, and she lost a little bit of her leg. But she had come back to work in a hospital. Maybe she walks with a limp, but she does work. I think she's a very brave woman to come back and battle again.

What if I said that you were a very brave kid?

I don't know. I'd think it's probably true. I'm just well-satisfied with myself. Well, of all things, I think I am a little gutsy, a little maybe.

Carl Hershey

I'm a hemophiliac. I'm missing something in my blood that makes it clot. I can't play rough stuff and everything because I don't have factor VIII in my blood like you do, and if I play a rough sport I'll get hurt. Like, if I get hurt the same way you do I'll get sore more than you will because I'm missing factor VIII and it takes me longer to heal. It's just a thing that I got and I can't play some of the things that you can play. I have to watch out for myself, so if I turn you down sometimes when you ask me to play something, now you know why. Not that I'm chicken or anything—I'm just watching out for myself.

When I'm hurt or something, when I'm sore and my blood count is low, then I go to the doctor and he gives me some factor VIII to help my blood clot. They take it out of whole blood and they give it to me intravenously. I just go whenever I'm sore—maybe once a month. I don't get sore that often, now that I'm older. I've got to where I can take care of myself but when I was younger I used to go quite a bit.

What kinds of things have you learned about taking care of yourself?

I know what I can do and what I can't do. Sometimes the things that I can't do I do anyway, and that's what makes me sore. Like I can't play tackle football or baseball—anything that pertains to roughness, or do lots of running and stuff like that. I get bruised or my joints get runny a lot and they get blood in them and they swell, just start getting swollen and sore when I can't move them. I can do things where I don't get banged around. Sometimes I can play touch football if I don't run a lot, and I like to do pool and stuff like that where you can't get hurt. That's one of my best sports, pool, and I can swim. The doctor said that that would be fine for my joints and that I wouldn't get sore and get banged around, so I will always be a swimmer.

Sometimes I do play basketball, football, or baseball. It aggravates me that I can't do what other kids do, because I want to and I think that I can. But if I try it afterwards I'm sorry for it cause I hurt myself; then I can't do something the next day, or when something comes up that's fun I'm messed up because I'm sore and I can't go. Sometimes I go out and I'll be trying to improve, and I'll get to where I forget to watch myself, then I'll start doing what everybody else does, just as much and as rough, and I get hurt.

Do the other kids, your playmates or whatever, give you any trouble?

Most of my friends know what I've got and know I can't do stuff and everything and they'll kind of watch out for me and I'll kind of let them know ahead of time, and if anybody really makes fun of me or anything then I just walk away and I don't really care what they think. It's what I think. If they laugh at me when I'm on crutches or I'm limping or something, I usually walk away and ignore them, but sometimes I'll fight back. I get so mad that I would like to haul off and knock somebody's head off or something. If I do, then they'll do the same thing thing to me and I'll just get hurt worse. But sometimes I just can't take it any longer and I'll just start fighting back for what I think is right. Like when bigger guys tease me and I'll say something back. Then when they want to fight I back off, and then I start getting scared because I think, wow, maybe they'll beat me up or something. And then I know that I should be careful and not fight back, and try to think of what I should do — either fight back and be sore or run and be scared — and sometimes I get confused and I don't know what to do.

But really I don't care what they say because I've been teased enough that I don't care. If I want to do it I'll do it and I don't care if anybody makes fun of me or says anything like, "Oh, you can't do it cause your leg is sore," something like that. I just do it if I want to, no matter what the kids say or anything.

But really the kids that make fun of me do it because they don't know what's wrong with me; if I really sat down and told them everything and they listened, they wouldn't make fun of me. With my friends, I'll sit down and tell them what's wrong and they'll say, "Well, I'll watch out for you and everything," and they do. And when their other friends make fun of me they will fight back for me and they'll tell them "Knock it off, because he's my friend; he's no different from you and I and it's just that he's got a problem and you don't." For awhile, I got pretty scared that if I told them what was wrong with me they wouldn't be my friend any more. So I wouldn't tell them and then I would get hurt and then they would start making fun of me when I was hurt and I couldn't do something; so then I thought that it's better to tell them than not tell them and get myself hurt.

I was going to the park one time and this kid asked me to play ball with him and some other guys and we played. Then I got hurt and I told him I couldn't play and he said, "Well, you can still play, it isn't very much." Afterwards I sat down and told him the whole story — what I can and what I can't do. And then he watched out for me and he would sometimes even tell me "You shouldn't do that." He wouldn't tease me no more or anything like that. I think it made him think about teasing people when they got a problem. Another time I was with this one kid and this bus drove by and he made fun of the kids in it because they had problems. And I told him about what was wrong with them and everything, and that he shouldn't make fun of them because it could happen to someone in his own family and then it would make him feel sorry for what he said about the other kids. And after that he never made fun of any kids any more, at least not when I was with him.

I'll be on my crutches sometimes and I'll be walking down the street, and people will get off away from me and walk around me instead of walking beside me because some people think that they might catch something. Nobody ever sat down and told them that they shouldn't be afraid of people with handicaps, that we are people just like them, except that we got a problem. When I'm walking on my feet, they just treat me like one of the gang, you know, but when I'm on crutches, sometimes they kind of ignore me and then I feel kind of left out and my feelings are hurt and I tell them where they went wrong and everything. It's not very fair to tease anybody or make fun of them cause they have a problem or they're on crutches or in a wheelchair or anything cause they're still a person.

When did you first realize that you had a problem with your blood?

I don't really remember when I realized that I couldn't do things. I guess when I was old enough to understand my mother told me, but I don't really remember — probably about seven or so, Mom figured that I was old enough to understand. She told me that I should take care of myself, because if I didn't I wouldn't be able to do things and go places because I would be sore. Now that I'm old enough to do that she doesn't have to, but she still does a little bit.

Now that I know what I can and can't do, and understand why I can't do things and why I can, she is not as worried.

How do you like school?

Well, every Tuesday I go to an art class for ceramics at an art center. I got a scholarship. I signed up for painting, and drawing but I was a little late on getting my interview so all that was left was ceramics and jewelry. And that's fun. Then every Friday at school I have oil painting class, me and some other kids. We were picked for that because we need stuff that's harder (not to be bragging), not the babyish stuff. We get kind of bored with that stuff that we do with the other kids because we're older and we draw a little better. If you're doing something that you like, then you want to do good in it, but if you're doing something you don't like and you're bored then you don't care. I look forward to every Tuesday and every Friday because of art. Art's my favorite subject.

Do you want to go into that when you grow up?

Yeah. But I'd rather be an architect than a painter. When you're an architect the things you make can be real, they can be made into something real that you can live in or ride in or something. But a painting, well, there's nothing else you can do with it except look at it. But if you're an architect you can make big things, like a house or something. I would like for people to know me and my work and to show everybody my work and everything. But when you're a painter, most of the paintings you do aren't successful; that's not true with the architect. Architects have a better chance, I think, than painters because you really have to make some beautiful paintings to be a great painter and have your name successful and everything. Besides that, architects make a lot of money. My cousin's an architect and he does freeways and everything. I enjoy drawing and art. Probably, if I get to become an architect, I'll do painting for a hobby.

Would you like it better if this school was combined with a regular school?

I'd like to go to regular school and not have to worry about some of the rules and regulations that they have here cause you get kind of tired of people bossing you and everything and you feel like you just have to go somewhere else and sometimes I feel that I got to go to another school cause I feel like everybody is on my back and stuff like that. Teachers and kids, and everybody, you know, and you feel like you got to go somewhere else. I have been going here for six years and it's a nice school and everything, but I wish that I could go to another school.

I think that when kids want to go somewhere else they should have the right to go wherever else they want, you know, to a special school or regular school. If they think that they can hack it, then their parents or whoever should let them. They're people too, they should have their rights too, and their say so. Parents, you know, they tell you what you can and what you can't do, still kids should be able to have their own say without getting their heads beat in or something like that.

How would you describe yourself?

I am just a normal person, only I have something that other people don't have. I'm smaller than some people and I'm bigger than some people, but I'm just a kid like every other kid. Everybody should be treated equal, whether they're a different color or they have a problem or they're a man or a woman or a boy or a girl, they should be treated equal.

Do you want to have kids?

If I get married. But I think that we should get to know each other first, and enjoy the good life, be able to, you know, go somewhere and not be tied down by kids and everything. So I don't think I would have kids right away if I got married. Sometimes when you have kids, and especially when they're little, you're tied down and you get kind of angry cause you can't do something. Some people regret having kids early, so that's why I think you should wait. Once you're older and know each other, then you can have kids and just enjoy each other.

Why do you say if you get married instead of when?

I don't really want to get married. I'd rather enjoy the bachelor life, have what I want and do what I want. If you want to go somewhere you can go, if you want to have something then you can have it, and there wouldn't be anyone to tell you not to or disagree with you. You can do what you want then, when you're alone.

Do you think your mother feels tied down at all?

I don't know. I don't care if she goes anywhere; I'm old enough to stay by myself and I don't feel jealous about it or nothing. She lets me go places so why shouldn't I let her go places. It's only fair. You shouldn't be jealous.

What would you like to tell handicapped kids and their parents?

Kids with handicaps are people too, so treat them like a person. Be cool to your kids. Just cause they got a problem it doesn't mean that they should feel sorry for themselves and be spoiled. If you really want to do something and you set your mind to do it you can do it and still be careful at the same time. I found that out. You shouldn't be too over-protective of your kids because that makes them dependent on the parents. Let them prove to themselves that they can do things without somebody helping them.

If you had a magic wand, what kind of world would you make?

A perfect one, where everybody is equal and the prices are lower. If I had a magic wand I would make people where they wouldn't have any problems and all the world would be one big happy family and everybody would be a person to each other and nobody would have hangups or nothing. If someone had a problem, you know, like being in a wheelchair and stuff, I'd make them just be a normal person, where they could walk and run and do whatever they wanted.

Anything else you'd like to say?

I think I said what I wanted to say. My mom told me especially not to mumble to myself and just to speak out and say everything I wanted to say, when you asked me questions to answer them clearly and answer them the way I feel. I feel that it's kind of an honor to be in a book.

Maria Sanchez

That Maria is included in these pages requires a word of explanation, for by all appearances she is able-bodied. That she made it at the end is due to a remarkable escape from the insituation which has branded her and society alike. Maria, then, carries the stigma of the social construction of handicap. She is included because she was treated *as disabled. She was placed in a large public institution with other people labeled handicapped, retarded, insane perhaps, because she came from a large Mexican family and her parents did not speak English. She may even be mildly retarded, but this would require access to privileged IQ tests because there is no indication that she is.*

Where Maria grew up is one of the more savage examples of a barbarous institution of human life. That places like it exist in our society is one of the blatant disgraces of the social construction of handicap. Currently there are moves to de-institutionalize. These moves are probably predicated more on saving money than on the welfare of the people involved. Be that as it may, change frequently makes room for improvement.

Maria is included here, then, because she suffered all or almost all the insults which society has for disabled people.

I was put in a state institution when I was four years old. I guess because my mother had a lot of kids—twelve altogether and we were too much trouble. She couldn't handle it. The Court put me there. And being put there really messed me up. When I really got serious, wondering what the heck I was doing there in the first place, and why my mother didn't want me and said I was

crazy, like I just got the feeling that I was, that I was retarded and all this stuff. When I was small I used to go to psychology and I'd see a bunch of people stand up in front and they would say, "Well, these people are retarded," and I learned this is what I was. I didn't know what that meant, crazy or slow, I didn't know the meaning of that. All I knew was that I thought I was crazy.

I said I was put in the institution, but at the time I didn't know who put me there. I always thought it was my mother. I loved my mother, but when she would call me crazy, then I really got mad, and I didn't know who to turn to. This is what really got me confused. I didn't know who to believe and who to love, and who loves me and all that stuff. So all of this really messed up my life completely. I grew up trying to think of what kind of person I am going to be. Am I going to make it in the world? Am I going to ruin my life, am I going to let it go on, am I going to be able to face responsibility for myself? I mean all these years, I never thought I'd make it because of the confusion of living at the institution, because of my mother, and all these feelings. I really didn't know what to do until I started finally taking responsibility, and seeing social workers, and going on psychology, talking to all kinds of people, and seeing what I really wanted out of life.

What are some of the things that you remember about living there?

When I first went there it was strange and kind of scary, because I had never been at a place like that. I was quiet for maybe two weeks or so, until I got used to the kids there and I could get friendly. But I got used to it and I guess I was getting along okay at that time. They used to take us out for walks and stuff, the attendants, play games and stuff.

As I got older I guess I got a little wise, and we used to get together, me and some other girls, and make our own little games up when the activities were over for the day. Sometimes they wouldn't be too nice a game. Us getting against girls, or girls getting against us, always trying to pick on somebody else. I used to enjoy it.

There were like a lot of girls that wasn't smart as we were, and they called them Mongoloids or low grades. We used to take certain girls for our friends. The others called them their pets, but

I always used to call them my friends. I didn't believe in calling them pet or baby and all that stuff. I liked this one little certain Mongoloid, and I used to give her candy, try to take from somebody else to give to her. This is what we would do to kill time and stuff.

It was fun, sometimes. We used to go out to the gym and ride bikes. They used to take us out to the circus. They used to have a band there and you'd go to rehearsal and then months later go out to perform, things like that. There were a lot of things that I really used to like. We had Girl Scouts and I was picked for a Brownie. So they had some things going on that I liked.

When I got older things got a little different. Now that I was on the big girls' ward I had to be a little careful of what I say, how to use my language, because I knew that I would get my butt kicked. If I was to get smart with some girls up there, or if I wanted to say a few things, tell the attendants where to go, stuff like that, that's how it would be. I got a little too smart, so I got transferred upstairs. Then upstairs I was kind of nervous and scared and wondering who I was going to talk to. You had to be a little more careful because if you got fresh with them, they'd show you where you belong. I was smart enough to know that, so I kind of stayed cool until I had gotten to know the girls and was able to stay with them.

There was like all different things changing. I had gotten to know more friends, and there was a little more pressure. We used to get into fights. Like I said, sometimes I would do things that I shouldn't be doing, like put somebody up to do something for me, then they'd tell on me because I put them up to do it. I used to take my shoes off and hit on the kids. People took me as a little big shot, and I used to tell people what to do. You see, people used to boss me so I got to do the same thing.

Did you ever see your parents?

They used to have visits on Sundays, and I used to hang around waiting and waiting for a visit every Sunday. Sometimes we would believe in this thing, we would cross our fingers and hope this day our mothers would come. And when our mothers would come we used to get so excited. We thought that this would be really good for us.

So my mother came like a couple of times for Easter and brought clothes, like nice dresses and shoes, and my father came, and the family, and she used to make chicken and stuff for us. And we used to eat, and I used to tell her what would happen on the ward and the type of things we do, and how I got into trouble and I used to get hit and all that stuff. After our parents left they would take the new clothes from us and write our names on the clothes and hang them up in the back and say, "Okay, you get to wear this the next time your parents come."

My sister lived there with me too. She was always the serious type, looking out for me and, well, I'm her little sister so she looked out for me, and she told me what was wrong and what was right. She would show me, take my hand and tell me this is what you should do. I used to make fun at people, and she said don't do that, it's not good.

We were really pissed off at my mother. We used to say, "What is Mommy doing, why do we have to stay here? We're not meant for this place." Sometimes she would stop coming to see us. And it was months and months and maybe a year or so, and we would write letters and try to get into contact with her. I'd get down, and my sister would tell me to cheer up and try not to let it worry me and stuff like that. We would get together and end up crying. Like it was always sad times, but I'm saying she was always around to help me.

She really talked to me. I was always joking around and playing around. I never really was as serious as she was. It was unusual, because she never liked playing as a little girl should. I tried to get her attention and play with her, and instead of playing, we would always get into arguments because she didn't like playing. So anyway, finally, I wised up, and I started really thinking strong. Like when she and I were there, we had I think maybe four or five brothers there too, and they got out. They made their way out because they proved they were smart and all that. One of them stayed. He had an eye problem. He couldn't see too well, and he had a hard time learning because of his eyes. I guess everybody thought that because he couldn't see he wasn't fast enough, and they figured he was retarded or something like that. But when we found out that my brothers got out, we really got disgusted and mad. We said if they got out why couldn't we?

So my sister really got me interested. She was talking about important things. She always looked into the future. She'd always say, "Don't you think that now that Mommy is not coming to see us we should talk to somebody to help us out or we should do something useful with our lives" or something like that. And then I started getting serious and I said, maybe we should. So we started getting stronger feelings.

I stopped the playing around and I got serious, and that meant that I lost a lot of friends that I had gotten close with. I got a little older and wiser. And I said, man, we're playing with our lives and we don't know what's what. They don't tell us stuff that we should know. I said, how the hell are we ever going to get out of here. We used to see kids go home and get visits all the time, so it used to really get us angry when our mother didn't come for a long time. We used to cry and get down, and say, "Man, when the hell is someone going to come see us?"

So, finally our mother came again. It was summer and we were outside and my sister got a rock thrown at her eye. My parents hadn't come in a long time and when they came and saw this happen they thought right away that this was meant. But it wasn't, it was an accident. A girlfriend threw it at my sister by accident. So my father saw it and he took it the wrong way. He couldn't control his temper and he threw chairs, and they said, look, if you don't stop we're going to call the cops on you and we're going to have to send your daughters back in and you can't see them for a certain length of time. So he got mad and he didn't listen.

A couple of times my father tried to sneak us home, because they wouldn't let us off the grounds to stay with our father. He took us home and we stayed for a certain amount of time and then we got tired of that, couldn't take it. Staying home, like we thought this was what we wanted, but it was just the same thing, only we were locked up even more. I can say one thing that was good about the institution — we had a lot of freedom and we were able to do more. When I was at home, we weren't even able to get out of the house. We were really busy the whole day. The whole day we never stopped, we just had to keep on and keep on and keep on working, and my mother always went out and my brothers never helped us, so it seemed like no one cared.

My mother was really religious and always went to church. Every time we went home, we went to church every night, for long hours, and I didn't like it. I just couldn't stand it. That wasn't my interest. I knew if I go home, I always had to go to church, or I always had to be in the house, and I didn't have time to play or nothing, so I felt like I was locked up at the institution and at home. If we didn't do what we were told our brother would hit us, things like that, and then we were called retarded from my brothers and my mother. Also, my mother sometimes didn't trust me and she used to hit me with the belts. I didn't feel like I was being loved. I thought I was getting mistreated all the time. So I said, I'm not going to be putting up with this.

So we were really confused when we found out how home was. I don't want to give the institution all the credit either, but at least they had clean linen and stuff, and you had something fresh to get into. And we thought that it was a lot more fun than staying home and being called this and that and getting whipped all the time. At least we had a chance to be able to go to school and learn a lot more because we still had so much to learn and catch up to.

I had no idea that this place could help us out with anything, because I just thought that it was a home for people who stayed there for good and that's that. If you had a family you could go with them, but that's it. Now I heard there were social workers there, but I didn't know what kind of help they give. I just thought that if a mother wanted to take children home, this is what they'll help them in. I never knew that they had anything else to do with us. So we had no choice. We stayed and we did the same thing. We had gotten so used to it that we got to like a few things there. But yet we cried. Our friends were leaving each year, going home for good with their parents and they would get more visits than us, and really a lot was happening to our friends. But all we would do was stay there and try to make more friends, and try to get used to the fact that we had to be there. We thought we had to be there the rest of our lives and rot. And I was really scared. I said, "Gee, now I can't go home. Now what are we going to do?" We always talked about it. But we just gave up.

How did you finally get out?

The doctor just decided it was about time that I get out.

When I first came out after all this mess, after all this confusion and stuff, I knew I had to start a life somewhere. But I'm still involved with this place.

All of my friends that used to be there, they're hardly there anymore. But I know some of the Mongoloids, and they remember me. They can remember when I was small, and I feel free with them, and they feel free with me. I went to see this girl I knew when I was small. But first I went to the attendant and I asked the attendant what she can do for herself. The nurse said, well, she's a good girl, but she's not able to hold a spoon well enough to feed herself. So what I did, I knew this girl, she's twenty-four now, I talked to her and she remembered me. I said, "How're you doing?" You know she's a Mongoloid and she talks well enough to get her by. I said, "Do you have any friends?" She said one friend. I asked her all these questions and then I took her to social service. She got excited because she went outside and I really got happy, because I seen her jump up and down, so I felt good because this is what I used to do. So I bought something for her to eat, just to see if she could feed herself well enough, and she does.

Most of the people that I talk with over there, the residents, they feel more free with me to come out with their problems. I tell them first thing that I would like them to have trust in me because whatever they tell me I won't go and tell anyone. I like to be trusted, I know how it is, so I make them feel comfortable enough to talk to me because I can understand. But I look at some residents, as they call them now, and I feel sad, I always feel like crying because I look back and it was good times and bad times.

What are you going to do in the future?

I'm thinking about getting married in a few years, but not now. I want to be able to take out some time for myself because later on I'll be having a lot more to do with my baby. She'll be getting older and there's a lot more things to run into, a lot more responsibility. I know that I should spend more time with her and then again I want to work, to be able to have things for her. I would like the baby to have the things that I never had, like attention. That especially, I'm still not able to give her as much attention as I should now that I'm working, but when I wasn't working, I gave her a lot of attention and tried to show her that I'm her mother and I want to be able to do as much as possible.

I was afraid to have a baby because I don't trust myself, I'm still a little uptight. I don't put myself down as much as I used to, and I don't look at life sad like I used to because now I accept myself for what I am, and now I say if no one else does, it's too bad. But what I'm saying is that I decided to have a baby because I wanted to see what kind of mother I would be and how much attention I would give to the baby. I would love to be able to do a lot more for that kid, to get to understand more of her feelings. Like I'm always thinking ahead of time, what would she be like when she gets older, what kinds of questions would she ask me? Suppose she asks me about my lifetime, what would she ask about my mother? And what would I tell her about my mother? How would I go about it? Things like that. If she has a tough time, I can try to explain why these things happen the way they do. I thought if I have a child, it would help me and it would help the child, like maybe this is what I want in life, to settle down and face responsibility.

Debra Hamilton

Debra uses a wheelchair. She works in state government. Her face, her manner, her speech were officially competent in the same way that one might expect to find many people's faces, manners and speech if they had official positions like Debra's.

But she had another side which started back in the countryside of her childhood, wove its way through her early development, the makings of her adolescence, the shaping of her education, and the formation of her adult person.

The experiences of people with disabilities are sometimes just different, sometimes funny, sometimes outrageous. I got to know Debra better a few months after we talked. We were in a van constructed to accommodate wheelchairs one afternoon around 2 o'clock. It was raining outside. Debra's sole entry to the building where we had an important appointment was blocked by a stalled truck. An hour later we were let off ten feet from an elevator. During the hour I had occasion to laugh and to get mad. And perhaps most of all to feel frustration. The frustration, I think, of being trapped.

We all take the fact that we can get from here to there for granted. We take prisons that prevent us from doing so very seriously and shortages in our supplies of gasoline which threaten to do so are no laughing matter either. Imagine if all of us had the same trouble in getting around as Debra. Now, more usefully, imagine solutions: widening a door here, installing a ramp there, and a hydraulic lift in between. And buses that "bow"; a car accessible for a wheelchair with a large rear door whose prototype lounges in a garage in England because there is no perceived market; wheelchairs, like Debra's, that are electric, wheelchairs, unlike Debra's, with range, speed and endurance.

Other disabled people may be otherwise handicapped with regard to transportation. One may not be able to drive. Another able to drive may find walking difficult. Another may have difficulty deciphering signs. To another verbal directions may be meaningless. And now constructively think of solutions. Many exist; many remain to be invented. Few are in place.

I'm twenty-seven and I work for the New York State Division of the Budget. I work fulltime on Section 504, which is part of the federal Rehabilitation Act of 1973. Section 504 says that all programs that receive federal money must be accessible to and usable by disabled persons, including people who are deaf, blind, or in wheelchairs. My role, along with my coworkers', is to provide technical assistance and guidance to state agencies in meeting the requirements of Section 504. Because there is no standard disabled person there is no standard solution, or standard service or modification that can be made in a program, and consequently the agencies have got to think through the different needs that different people may have. I think what's important for a state agency is to have the awareness, the concern, and the desire to fulfill the civil rights spirit of the law so that the agency can bend, be flexible, do whatever is required so that individuals can use the various programs, services, and benefits of the state agency, as anyone else can. It's difficult because state agencies are bureaucracies, and they want to do things by rule, by memos, by directives, by fixed formulas, and a law like 504 says that you have to rethink the way that you provide some of your services. So that's a real challenge and in some cases it makes a difficult problem for any agency.

It sounds like a big job. Why should they be bothered with it?

The job of state agencies is to serve the public, I mean it's as simple as that. They are there to provide various kinds of programs to meet people's needs. 504 simply reiterates that they have to serve all the public.

It's essentially a civil rights law—I think that's the way it's perceived by both the advocacy groups and the State of New York—and it needs to be enforced that way. If an individual has a complaint of discrimination against a state agency, an attempt is made to resolve it within the agency; all agencies now have an affirmative action officer and a 504 coordinator. And disabled rights have been incorporated into other civil rights procedures for the state, as well.

Is it difficult to get individuals and state agencies to comply with 504?

Probably the real crunch that you get into working on 504 on a day to day basis is that you are trying to persuade people to comply, trying to draw out their better instincts, whatever you want to call it, but sometimes you do have to say it's the law, it's a right, and it will be done. And that's a tough situation. It's always preferable I think to have somebody on your side, and to have somebody working toward the same goals as you are, because they *want* to, and it's nice to know that you don't have to drag anyone screaming and kicking into 504, but that they understand it, they agree with it, they believe in it, and they're going to do it because they want to do it. When that happens there's a lot more positive energy directed toward solutions. Also, I think that the public's needs will be better met when that happens. On the other hand, there's the reality that it's difficult to budge not only state agencies but individuals. They may be jaded by having to deal with all sorts of federal regulations and they may see this as just another one, particularly when it comes down to the money problems. It's an easy excuse for people to say, well we just don't have the money to do it.

I think one of the major problems at first was understanding what program accessibility is about. The initial reaction was, well we've got to put up $50,000 elevators in every building—we have to tear down the world and rebuild it to be architecturally accessible. That isn't of course, what the regulations call for. Agencies are just beginning to understand and realize that they have to internally review their programs and their services so that they can be used by people with all sorts of disabilities, not just by someone who is in a wheelchair. If an individual is deaf or blind or has some other type of disability that requires modifications that are nonstructural or nonarchitectural, an agency has to be just as ready and able to do that as putting in ramps and elevators.

In addition, agencies need to examine how they interact with

the public. One of the things that I really see a strong need for is training the front-line people—the people who are really providing the services, the people who are really meeting the public—so they understand what 504 is about. The actual interaction of a state agency and the public happens at the individual level—between a receptionist and someone coming into the office asking a question, or between a case worker and someone in need of some sort of service. I mean, it's easy to set up a task force, to set up a committee within an agency, and say o.k., this is how we see things happening. But in reality it's very difficult to control the actual individual interaction between someone who's working for the state and someone who comes to that agency to use a program.

Do you think 504 is working?

We are definitely making progress toward 504's working in this state. I am convinced that there are people who are genuinely committed to it and who still have enthusiasm for it even after this time. But it may not be working in the sense of the hopes of a lot of people when it was first signed—I don't think we are seeing some of the major changes that we perhaps expected from it—but maybe over time... The hopes of a lot of people were that buildings would become architecturally accessible by 1980 and there would be sort of a whole spirit attached to the thing and I don't think there is that kind of excitement and hopes and dreams sort of thing attached to it. I don't think what is happening in 504 is comparable to the public awareness that happened with the civil rights acts for blacks and other minorities, or with the women's movement. I don't know whether that's a media thing, whether disabled persons haven't been visible enough in the whole process to get that kind of excitement going or generated. But I don't think that means it isn't working. I think there's movement, forward movement on it, and progress, but it's not meeting the expectations many disabled people originally had.

I think one of the things that has been holding 504 back, without any doubt, is the lack of commitment of money from Washington to work on it. In working at the state level, talking to people from other states, I've seen that for many states the fiscal situation is so tight that they haven't made the commitment of money that I think there should be. Yet there hasn't been any help from Washington either. There have just been regulations promulgated, and the states have just been told, you should do this. There's been little guidance and little dollars and cents help to do it. But that's no excuse for a state not to do something about 504. The question, I guess, is how much the states can contribute, and at what point should they have a right to expect some help from the federal government.

I think, too, that when there's some money coming out of Washington it says to the states that there is a commitment, that it is a national priority and we're serious about it. When there isn't some money involved, there's a certain assumption, there's a certain implication it's not as important as some other things.

I don't know what the mood is in other states on 504, but I really do think that there's some commitment to it here in this state—and I'm not just saying that because I'm being paid off by the state. I'll tell you some of the reasons that I feel there is some commitment. The Governor has a history of being involved in these issues when he was in Congress, and I think he does have a concern for trying to do what 504 requires. And secondly, the state has put up money for it. I don't know how many other states have done that. But we have separate lines in the state budget to make architectural modifications to comply with 504, and I think that says something. By the time we get this on paper, we could say that for last year and this year nearly seventeen million dollars has been spent by the state for barrier removal. Though the job isn't finished, that's a significant commitment to 504. I don't know if there's that much happening in other states.

What else could be done to make 504 work?

Well, for one thing I would like to see the courts interpret 504 consistently. I think there's been quite a lot of confusion on that end. I'd like to see disabled consumers better informed on what 504 means and involved in making it happen in their own communities; 504 isn't something that will happen only from the top down. I think there needs to be a lot more attention paid to what's happening right in our own backyards, so to speak. Realistically that's where people can probably make the greatest difference and actually see the results the best.

Why do you see 504 as a civil rights issue?

As I said earlier, all members of the public should be able to use agency services and programs. As taxpayers, everyone has the right to expect that. We pay for programs, we pay for services state agencies provide, and everyone should be able to use them. To me that's pretty simply and basic.

Some have claimed that disabled people don't pay as much in taxes.

If that's true, there are some pretty obvious reasons. People with disabilities haven't had the opportunity to get employment, to be independent, because government agencies have not served them in the same way that they've served the rest of the public. The same job opportunities haven't been there. Services, such as transportation or housing, have not been made available to people with disabilities to the same extent that they've been made available to the general public. In many ways government has contributed to and sometimes even created the problem. Now through 504 we've got to solve it.

I operate under the assumption that it's obvious that we're talking about civil rights. I see definite correlations between 504 and other civil rights statutes, although in some cases 504 may not be as strong as some of them. I don't know how you could look at 504 if you didn't see it as a civil rights statute. To look at it in any other way would suggest to me that disabled people are somehow different from the general public. I think it's very basic that we're talking about civil rights. 504 says that disabled individuals should have equal opportunity to use the programs and services that the general public uses. It's an issue of having rights … of someone disabled having the same rights and opportunities as anyone else. I don't believe that those rights and opportunities have been in the past. 504 attempts to address civil rights issues: access to programs, access to services, equal opportunity in employment.

Probably a lot of people see it in more of a social services sort of way. How can we provide something for disabled people? How can we do better? I guess maybe for me the civil rights part of it has certain assumptions about attitudes attached to it; it assumes that someone who is disabled has the same rights to use the service as anyone else, and that it's not a question of an agency trying to do its best. The issue is that the agency has to provide it.

Do you feel some sort of political organization of disabled people is necessary?

I think that's important because that keeps the pressure on government if disabled people are organized to the point where they will go to the courts to enforce 504. It's probably especially important in view of the fact that there hasn't been as strong action out of Washington as there might be on it, particularly in terms of committing some money to it. It's like anything else. State agencies, any government agency will have to budge if they are made to by the public. If consumer groups can create that sort of pressure from the outside they get immediate attention. It just all the more says to government agencies that this is a serious law and you will have to comply with it.

My impression has been that consumer involvement with 504 has been kind of spotty. In certain issues like transportation there's been very intense involvement on it; on other issues there's been less pressure from advocacy organizations. I don't know whether that will change or not. I don't know whether organizations of disabled people will push 504 to where it should be going or whether they will assume that it's already being done. I think that kind of pressure from the outside is definitely needed.

How did you end up taking this job?

I had worked on 504 at the State University of New York in Albany—I was a grad student there and had been involved in the task force that had been set up to look at the University's programs and services—so, I had pretty good familiarity with 504. I also happened to be on a Civil Service list, which was timely for me because when I graduated, the budget division was looking for additional people to work fulltime on 504. So I was eligible by virtue of being on the Civil Service list, and I also had some understanding of it.

I think that my being disabled had a certain appeal to filling the position. From the Division's point of view, I suspect that it lends a little bit of credibility to what I do. I hope it does. By experience I know quite a lot about what program modifications would be needed, and you can't teach that in a day to someone who isn't disabled. While I attended the University, I worked part time in the disabled students' office, so in addition I gained some knowledge about what sort of modifications in programs someone who is blind or deaf might need. While I'm not an expert on that subject, I think I have at least enough understanding to be able to know whether a state agency proposal is really going to solve a problem, meet a need, or not.

Is there any connection in your own head between your being disabled and having this job?

In terms of attitude there very much is. I have a personal interest in it no doubt. I want to be able to use state services and programs as much as someone else. I want to be able to use state parks. I want to be able to use transportation services that the state provides or subsidizes or is in some way involved in. I very definitely have a self-interest in it.

And in terms of attitudes, I think I have a kind of approach I hope will influence the way administrators and state agencies will attempt to implement 504 — in terms of not taking a paternalistic sort of attitude, or an attitude of we'll try to help these people, but instead an attitude of we have to provide these services because everyone has a right to them. That's the only way I can interpret 504. So I hope that I project the attitude that this is a right that people have, that people can expect under the law.

I've talked to a few people on the phone who haven't known that I was disabled and they've said, we don't know what to do with this law, and, we've tried our best and we just don't see what else we can do besides what we're doing now, what do people expect? What more can we do? These people don't understand the problem that we have and that kind of thing. When they find out that I'm disabled they probably understand that no state administrator is going to cry on my shoulder about how hard it is for them to do 504. I can't say, there, there, I know you've got real problems and I know people are just expecting too much from you and too much of your agency. I have to say, we've got to be a little more creative about this. O.K., we've got money problems. Let's sit down together and see how we might attack it, how else we might solve it. And I can say, yes, I think you're moving in the right direction of this, or no, that's not the right direction to go but we can try to be creative.

There's a solution, a way to solve a lot of the access problems that agencies feel. But there is a real lack of knowledge, besides attitude problems, that we run into. There is a lack of information, lack of understanding that can start an agency down the wrong path in terms of trying to implement 504. For example, I think for a lot of people, their first reaction to making a program accessible is to make a separate program. They will want to hire specialists of all kinds and rehab counselors. Their intentions are good. It's difficult, but you have to say to people like that, that's not what 504 is about. And you have to make them understand that they are separating people with disabilities from the rest of the public. They're reinforcing the same kinds of attitudes that have kept disabled people out of agency programs in the past.

So you have some degree of power, right?

Well, the Division is one of the control agencies, you could say, in state government, along with agencies like Civil Service and Audit and Control. We do have some degree of authority in terms of being able to direct agencies down one path or another. I think the tack the Division has taken on 504 is that we aren't the compliance people for 504—Washington is. Instead, we've played more of a coordinative role, an informational role.

To some extent we do monitor what's going on in the state. For instance, we look at the transition plans and self-evaluations put together as required by 504. We try to give the agencies some feedback on what kinds of directions they're taking—positive, negative. If there's a real conflict in the way that I or my coworkers might interpret 504 and the way that someone in a state agency is interpreting it, it will be resolved in the governor's office. Fortunately, we haven't come up against those kinds of situations because by and large agencies haven't been going out on their own. They've wanted to talk with other 504 coordinators and other agencies. They'll call and say, we've got this as an idea. Are we thinking along the right track? Is it in line with 504? Will it solve a need or is it the wrong approach? So I really act more in that kind of a role. When I see a problem I can flag it, though, and say, there's something here that doesn't comply with 504 and we're going to have to talk about it. We can say to an agency, we anticipate that this is going to be a problem, that you may not get through a compliance review. And then we work to find a solution.

Tell me a few things about your personal life.

Well, let's see. I grew up on a farm in the Northeast. I have a younger sister and brother who aren't disabled. My parents, I think, are terrific people. I was raised with the assumption that I could be anything I wanted to be. There were one or two kids in my high school who were disabled, and they seemed to function the same way I did—which was independently. Back then, you didn't think about the kids who couldn't function independently, if you even knew they existed.

I went through public schools all my life because my parents insisted on it. The school district said, we don't know how we're going to get her into the building or we don't know how we're going to get her up to the science lab, and my parents would say, we feel she should be able to go to public school and would you work out a solution? This was before there were laws that schools now have to comply with. In most cases the administrators made the schools accessible for me.

I think that was important. I didn't realize it until I met a number of disabled people in college who hadn't gone to public school. They had been shunted into special ed classes and separate schools when they really didn't need it. A lot of times they came from suburban areas where the school districts have special programs which the smaller schools that I went to never did. So in a sense that was an advantage for me. To travel to a special education program would simply not have been possible. It would have been too far away. So I went to the local schools, although I suspect that had there been a whole lot of alternatives, the schools would have been able to more strongly insist that there be some sort of other education for me. But there really weren't any other opportunities. And my parents felt strongly that I should be in public schools and we were always able to work it out that way. I think it was real important for my being able to learn how to cope with a disability, how to be a "regular person."

I don't know how the other disabled kids grew up, but I think my family was really terrific. I was always part of whatever we did—summer vacations, traveling, the whole thing. I was never treated any differently. As the oldest child I even have the classic syndrome in terms of the achievement bit! My sister and brother are both probably considerably less competitive than I am. I have terrific relationships with them, too, and as adults we enjoy each other very much. I think I had an almost idyllic childhood—riding on haywagons and the whole bit. It's almost corny the way I grew up on a farm. But it was really a great experience. I was able to be outdoors, and now I think I'm very much in touch with the outdoors. This summer in fact I got into camping, sort of took that up as a new thing. My passion now is to camp during the summer.

I can identify pretty specifically a point in my life in college where I became aware of the movement, you could call it. Up until that point I really never thought of myself as being different. It's funny how you can grow up being disabled and somehow not be that much aware of it. I knew there were certain things I couldn't do that other kids could do. But in general, I didn't have any understanding of concepts like prejudice, or that people might not let me be what I wanted to be.

College, again, was a positive experience. I went to a small liberal arts school, which was pretty much accessible. I was the second student there in a wheelchair. The school was very positive about accepting disabled students, definitely one of the first schools in this area that really recruited students with disabilities and made an effort to make the college experience a good one. I lived in the dorms while I was going there, and made a lot of very good life long friends that I keep in touch with.

At some point there was a terrific guy, who now works in Washington, who would come around in his wheelchair trying to get together a local committee on the disabled in Dutchess County. He would come around and try to get me involved in this thing, to come to some meetings. He even got a woman to come up from New York City and talk to us, although only five or six people came to the meeting. She's very well known in the movement now. But I was totally out of touch with that back then. I was having a good time, partying at school and the whole thing. Mike would say, come on, come to the meetings. And I would just feel like, oh, god, not again. I would go because he was a friend, but I really wasn't into it, really wasn't concerned.

I think the point where I started to become politicized in a way was through reading some of the advocacy magazines I would pick up in the office that was set up for disabled students. Before that I'd been pretty much on my own in getting them to take a door off the bathroom stall or something like that I needed. It really blew my mind when I started reading the magazines in my last year at college, and started to realize that there were thousands and thousands of people across the country who were dealing with some of the same situations that I was. It was really a turning point for me.

It was very exciting. I think probably by nature I am a political person. I like group action. I like to be involved in organizations that are doing things. I like to be involved with change. I see a lot of social situations as challenging things that need to be changed. What happened for me was that I became aware that the things that I faced as personal barriers were social barriers, that I wasn't the only person that had to deal with a flight of steps, or who had to deal with trying to explain to a prospective employer why I felt I could do the job. And I started to see what it meant in a broader context, in terms of the kind of political action that would be required to change those things. It was a real turning point for me in terms of understanding where I was in the world, and understanding what kinds of barriers I was going to have to face.

I was fortunate to find a job working at a Head Start center. I started as a volunteer and then made it into a summer job while I went to college. It was an interesting experience because I became aware of some of the government programs and community action sort of things. Then I took a job when I graduated with a local organization called the Task Force for Child Protection, which was committed to child protection programs, preventing child abuse and neglect. That job was another real turning point and awareness-raising experience for me because I became aware of advocacy—what it meant, how to do it at a local level. We were doing it in the field of child protection but I think there's a lot of carryover just in terms of the general concept. And I also became aware of the role of government in all sorts of social programs. At college I'd majored in psychology and thought that I might want to go into being a counselor or something like that, helping people deal with their individual problems. But working at the Task Force and also understanding how Washington and

Albany and county government impact on the problem of child abuse, how money flowed to programs or didn't flow to programs, the patterns of control between different levels of government, just opened up a whole new understanding for me of the way government affects people. It really turned me on to a broader way to attack social problems. So I became interested and fascinated by government early on and how it worked and how it affected social problems.

I decided after working at the Task Force for a little over a year and a half that I wanted to go to grad school and try to get a handle on all these new insights that I'd had through working there, and also get a degree so that I could go into the kinds of work that I was projecting myself into and seeing myself doing, which was working in government in the human services area. I was very fortunate to find a program up here. The University was probably the most accessible, certainly in this general area. Another drawing card for me to come up here was the fact that it was the state capital. I was looking for a place where I felt I could get involved politically with my interest in impacting on social problems, and this seemed the right environment for it. Politically, educationally, architecturally, everything about it was pretty good. When I chose my field work assignments I very consciously aimed toward places where I felt I could learn how the political system operated, and also learn something about all the new things going on, like 504.

My first field work assignment I had to do a litle dealing with the school to get. I proposed it to the school, figuring if I didn't go where I wanted to go they'd put me where they wanted to put me. I found out who was doing the White House conference planning for the State of New York, and I approached him and asked if he could use a grad assistant, and he said terrific. The school accepted my proposal and I spent two semesters learning a lot about state government. And I learned a lot about the movement in the sense that I had a lot of contact with advocacy organizations around the state and met a lot of disabled people who had their heads very much together on the kind of issues that the White House conference was dealing with.

The second year I asked to be placed with the legislature. It didn't deal very much at all with 504 but I wanted to learn how that system operated. I can't say I especially enjoyed the time that I worked there but I definitely learned a lot from it. The atmosphere of the legislature is a very fast paced, almost scatter shot way of dealing with issues and just wasn't an environment that I felt particularly effective or comfortable in. I knew that I'm more of a program kind of person anyway and wanted to go into something in the executive branch. I like a situation where I can dig into something, get to know a program, get to know an issue, and get to apply myself to it. In the legislature they simply don't attack any one problem with that kind of an approach. There's just too many things going on there for very much attention to any one thing. But I went in there to learn, because you obviously have to impact on that system if you want to make any sort of political gains or have any sort of political goals.

While I was going to grad school I was working parttime for the University's rehabilitation service, and doing a little bit of counseling for disabled students. It was a job, but it wasn't only for the money. It was also because I go buggy after a while if I'm alone with the books and I have to have some sort of involvement beyond the academic life. That was probably as much an education experience as going to school was in a lot of ways. I got involved with the school's administration, some of the deans, and understanding how the University operated as a political body in a lot of ways. Also, I became more familiar with disabilities other than my own — which for the record is amyotonia. It's a muscular disability which I was born with, so I've always used a wheelchair. By working at Rehab Service with students who were blind, or who had hearing impairments, my own awareness of what disability meant to different people was broadened. And I also got involved with the 504 process at the University.

From what I've seen from other schools, the University at Albany really took a positive approach in doing something with 504. They aren't by any means the best or ideal model, but I think they've had a history of being concerned and providing access for disabled students to the campus and educational programs. They were comfortable with getting disabled students involved. My second and last year there, I was president of the disabled student's group — University Action for the Disabled. We had very good involvement in the whole 504 process. We did a transition plan and self-evaluation. We met the deadline. Not too many schools did that. It was a good learning experience. It was just a good positive experience in terms of seeing what I'd have to say were good attitudes on the part of most people there. You run across individuals in any situation who are paternalistic or are wringing their hands trying to figure out what in the world they can do to comply with 504. But I think in general, the people that I met at the University were coming from a good place and in the right way. That was where I did my time with 504 as far as learning about that. After that it was to the Division of the Budget. So that's a quick history.

I don't know whether I'm always going to want to work in government. What I'm doing right now is very rewarding and I feel like I can make a difference. But I don't believe in staying in any one position or spot for too long a time. I think there's something to learn in every place and there's something you can contribute to it. Sometimes the position evolves and becomes something new from when you started and you can stay with it; other times if the situation stays the same and you evolve, you have to move on to something else. In the future I could move into several different areas. I'm very interested in independent living and could see myself getting involved in that. I could also see myself moving into teaching in some way, but always staying in touch with the movement because I feel very connected to that.

We have a local organization, Wheels to Independence, that was organized in 1972. I'm very involved in that on the local level as a private citizen. We aren't shattering any great myths in Albany and we're not shaking the earth here by any means, but we're having some impact. We've worked with our Mayor to plan curb cuts in the city of Albany and to study housing and other needs of people with disabilities in this area. We've also just begun an independent living program that we're very excited about. In small organizations like ours, you sometimes wonder if anyone else is doing anything, or if you're doing all the work yourself! But everybody has those feelings and knows those kinds of frustrations. I think it's important to be organized, to work with an organization, and to have contact with other people who are facing the same sorts of barriers that you're facing. You can support each other.

My own commitment to civil rights carries over in terms of private life and my job, my public role, whatever. I hope that I'm sensitive to not only civil rights as it affects people with disabilities, but as it affects all groups that have advocated for their rights in the past several years. I see a connection between my job and my involvement in Wheels to Independence. What I've learned is one has been important to the other, both ways. I hope I've been able to combine experience in government with an understanding of what's really happening in people's lives as they deal with barriers.

I went from understanding my own situation, I went from seeing the barriers that I face, to understanding the broader social forces at work around me, and I think I was able to do that through my jobs in a lot of ways, and through my college experiences. My perspective was broadened and I started to realize that it wasn't just me facing a particular barrier on my own—that barrier existed not only for me but for many other people with disabilities. That barrier wasn't just in the particular locality that I happened to be living in but it was all over the country. The only way to deal with something that large was through organized activity and through political action and a great many disabled people came to realize that. I suspect that probably most people who are involved in the disabled rights movement at some point went through that evolution themselves—went through that change of understanding. I'm sure I'm not unique by any means in having had that experience. It's probably a necessary experience if you are to become involved in the movement—you don't get into the movement unless you go through that change in awareness.

I terms of my private life, in terms of my friends, I don't talk about work—very rarely. They'll ask me sometimes what's going on. Built any ramps lately? That kind of thing. I'll talk about it. Somehow to them, they sort of knew me before I got politically involved in all this sort of stuff. But they know me as an individual. I'm more than a political person obviously. With friends, especially the ones who are able-bodied, I'd rather not talk about disabled anything. Their company is the chance to be the other things that I am. In the summertime, I'm into going up to the woods and camping and traveling and doing things that have nothing to do with advocacy. I find that I need to do that, I need to get away from it a lot of times.

There's a certain point where sometimes you can feel that you're becoming a symbol instead of a person. At least I feel that. When you're living day in and day out with civil rights issues and the movement and advocacy, you can after a while feel like what you are is a disabled person instead of a person. That part of my life, which will always be a *part* of my life, can feel like it's taking over sometimes. The other interests that I have and the other things I like to do can seem to go by the way. So, I consciously take time out and put the advocacy thing aside. For me that's important.

In my job I play that symbol very much. Probably a lot of people do who are disabled and who are involved with this in some way through a job. On the job you are a disabled person. It's important to try to make people that I work with in other agencies, people that I'm dealing with day in and day out, realize that I am not some sort of a standard disabled person either. What I might need isn't what somebody else needs. To get them to broaden their perspective, to see beyond me to the rest of the disabled community, is something I hope I get across.

I am working from within the system. There's no doubt about that. I'm not making political decisions that affect 504 in the state. There are many of those to be made, but policymakers will be making them. I think I can help form policy on many issues by contributing my point of view and knowledge, but realistically it's other people who will make the real decisions on 504. I don't have delusions of grandeur in that sense.

But it makes me feel good in that I think I can have some impact. I feel that I can make a difference with the job I'm in and in the way state agencies will meet 504, and I have to admit that I'm glad that I'm in that position. I think my being there does make a difference. I'm really convinced that when agency administrators interact with disabled people who know their rights and expect to be treated as equals, that the administrator's own attitudes are changed for the better, they understand 504 better, and they will on their own make the right decisions.

Brenda Clark

It's hard to tell why one person makes it and another doesn't, surely as hard for the handicapped people as for able-bodied people. With Brenda there are some clues. She came from a large family and lived close to other people. These "support networks" nourished her and asked that she nourish them. But she had to overcome many socially constructed obstacles. She was handicapped, black, a woman, a single mother, and poor. Can it be that these variables play themselves out differently with a handicapped person? Or is Brenda exceptional?

Brenda has little use of her arms. When she walked into the room she took off her jacket with her mouth. It turned out that she did most everything with her mouth. The pen she grasped with her teeth wrote elegantly. The baby whose Pampers she had changed, whom she had fed, whose bed she had made with her mouth was pictured in a family album, now, looking happily toward the future.

I'm twenty-six years old. I've had polio since I was seventeen months old. I was unable to walk for a number of years. However, while I was in the hospital I was given physical therapy and improved a lot. So I can walk now. At one time I wore two braces, then only one. I was wearing a long leg brace on my right leg for about twenty-four years. But I don't wear that now. I'm unable to use my left arm at all. I can use my right arm but only to an extent, like I can't open some doors, I can't lift things that are too heavy, I can't grasp anything. I can't do such things as my buttons, or tie my shoes. Sometimes I can use a pen or pencil to zip my pants or if I'm wearing a jacket that zips I sometimes zip it half way then step into it and zip the rest of the way.

What are you studying here at the University?

Well, my major is sociology. This semester I have four courses: sociology, women's studies, urban politics, and I take a mini-course in law and justice called Law and the Disabled.

After I got out of high school I had no real intention of coming to college. I had always been in business courses and I really thought that I wanted to be some kind of secretary or work in an office setting. But even before I graduated from high school I had worked a couple of years in different offices, and I just didn't like it. I liked my boss and the people that I worked with, but it wasn't really the type of work that I wanted to do. What I feel I would like to do is either work with handicapped individuals or with abused children and their parents. I'd like to give some kind of counseling to children and parents.

How important was your family to you in dealing with your disability?

I think it was very important. While I was growing up I felt that we were very, very close. Although my father didn't live with us I'm still close with him, and my stepfather lived with us for a while when I was small. There were eleven in the family. One of my brothers died a few years ago and that was a great loss to me. He was murdered and it was just a big emotional thing for the whole family, which brought me closer to the rest of my family.

I think that I show my family a lot of love, and I think that they know that I would do anything I could for them. I'm always trying to do little things to help my mother out—like if she needs something, I try to help her—because I feel that my mother was just a great person to have kept me. A lot of parents don't even want to keep their children after they have some kind of birth defect. I really feel grateful to her for being able to struggle with me in and out of the hospital and through operations and stuff. I know that her prayers and just being there with me was a great help to me. She used to give me physical therapy at home on the kitchen table, and I know that helped me. And it was a long way from her home to the hospital, but she always made it her business to get somebody to bring her out there or come out her-

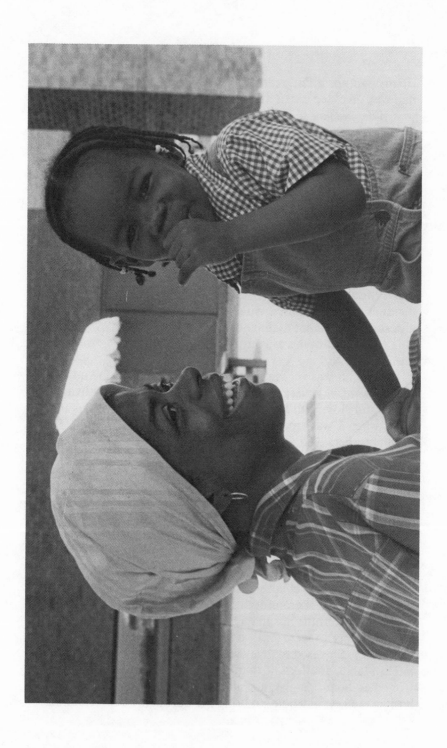

self in a cab or whatever. To have as many kids as she did, I think that was a lot of strain on her, and I feel grateful now that she was able to do it. I appreciate her and love her a whole lot for doing it for me.

What was it like when you first got polio?

I was in an iron lung for a long time. I can't remember too much when I was small but I do remember being in the hospital for a number of years. I used to just come home on weekends. I remember being out there for a long time and going through lots of different operations—mostly for my right leg. I went to school out there for a little while, maybe a year. Other than that I believe I was at the Industrial School for Crippled Children, which is a school for handicapped and disturbed kids. It was okay, but I think as I began to grow up and notice myself and realize the problems that I had, I began to resent the school. I felt I was being confined. For some reason I didn't like going to school with everybody in the class having some kind of a disability. I felt underpriviledged or something. When I was about in the eighth grade I discontinued going there and I believe I had a tutor for one year. And then I went to public school, where I knew a lot of people. Three of my older sisters and brothers had been students of that school and I just felt that I wanted to be one of those students myself. I felt good graduating from a school like that.

Were you accepted on a social level at school?

I always had plenty of friends in all the schools I went to, and I still see some of those friends now. I've always been able to meet and socialize with people fairly well. I do sometimes find it difficult to deal with my handicap when I go out to a nightclub. Sometimes I feel a little funny. But I think lately since I've been getting involved with different organizations and really talking with other disabled people, I've been more aware of myself mentally and physically so I can do a lot of things now that bothered me before—like asking someone to take my coat off if I'm in a club. I would feel really funny asking someone to do that for me. But now I'd rather just ask somebody to help unless I feel like being bothered with going through all the motions myself.

There have been times when I felt lonely and was very depressed and I just felt like I was a crippled person and nobody

liked me and nobody cared about me. I had all those feelings that
I'm sure a lot of other handicapped people have had. But I think
what helps me is coming from a large family. I talk quite openly
with people and, I don't know, there just used to be people that
interested me. Different males took an interest in me and I liked
them. Sometimes people have been turned off to me because of
the fact that I'm disabled, and other times people have told me
they like me because I'm disabled, because I have a sense of
feeling that maybe an able-bodied person might not have.

I used to worry too that I might not be able to have any kids.
But my doctor said, sure you can have children, it wouldn't be
any problem at all. I just felt that one day I would like to experience that feeling, and that I would like to have the responsibility of raising my own child. Now I have a daughter — she'll be
two next month. She weighed six pounds and twelve ounces when
she was born. She's been a great thing for me. Beautiful little girl.

I wasn't worried at all. I was very happy. I had a few personal problems between myself and my boyfriend. But other than
that I had a really beautiful pregnancy. I wasn't sick during it or
anything. It was really good. It was nice.

The first time I felt my daughter move inside me, I was so
excited. I just sat around and waited for her to move. Then when
she was really growing faster and my stomach was sticking out,
she used to kick a lot. She used to always kick me and I could just
see her little feet or hands poking out of my stomach. She was
very active inside.

Before my daughter was born, I used to think very seriously
about how I was gonna take care of her, because I knew that my
mother thought that I wasn't gonna be able to take care of her
and she was worried about how I would pick her up, how I would
change her diapers, how I would feed her, how I would burp her.
You know, how would I do all those things that needed to be
done for her that were so very important?

When my baby was born I breast-fed her for like five days
and then I kinda punked out of that situation. So I switched to
formula and just fed her out of the bottle. I went to my mother's
for the first two months, and I paid one of my sisters to wash and
sterilize the bottles for me. All the other things I did myself. I
could change her diaper with my mouth and my right hand. I sat

her on my lap and fed her. And to burp her, I would kind of have her head propped up on my shoulder and I would pat her back with my chin. She was a good baby because she used to always burp about two or three times, so there was no problem there.

When I had to pick her up to take her out of the bed to change her sheet or to change her clothing, I would lay her on a receiving blanket and I would take each of the corners together, pull them together, and pick her up with my teeth. She was always secure inside the blanket and I would take her from her crib and put her on my bed which was just a space away from the crib. And I could change her clothes all with my mouth. As she got bigger and bigger it became harder and harder, you know, so when she was about five months I started changing her diaper with my feet. I would put her down on the floor on her blanket, or I could do it on the bed, and I would change her with my feet. I could wash her up with my feet. And I used to do just about everything with my feet or with my mouth and the use of my one hand. I dressed her and I brushed her hair with my mouth. And, let's see, I just did everything! I could fix her formula and everything. I shook up the cans of Similac, and opened 'em up. I fed her baby food and cereal... I do all my cooking with my mouth. You know, it was something that I just had to do for my daughter.

I also wouldn't allow anybody to just pick her up and hold her and rock her or anything like that unless it was absolutely necessary, which it never was. That was because I couldn't just pick her up at any time. I knew it would be a hassle for me to go in there and pick her up or try to carry her around with me during the day and stuff. She crawled and walked really early. She used to pull up in her bed and stand up all the time, you know, because she really never got a lot of that picking up, which I think sometimes makes kids lazy when they know somebody's gonna just come over and pick 'em up and hold 'em. I mean, it's comfortable to be picked up and held—you can relax and not really want to pull up on your own. But when you see everybody doing something in another part of the room and you're just lying in the crib, if you want to do something you're gonna have to get up out of the crib.

She's an active little girl. She does everything. She's just beautiful. And she's smart. She unzips my jacket and takes it off for me. She puts things in the dishwasher. She tries to clean up her room. She's potty trained since she was about fourteen or fifteen months. She doesn't wet the bed or anything. She's really good. She's a good little girl. She feeds herself. She can dress herself. I'm trying to get her to learn how to tie her shoes and stuff now. She can't quite button. She can zip things up and down but she can't poke the little zipper inside the clasp. But she does really, really good.

How do you show her how to do these things?

I can't show her myself but my mother and my sisters and other people show her. She tries to copy how I do things sometimes. When I'm making my bed I usually pull the covers up and try to straighten them with my teeth and I pick the pillows up with my mouth. One day I told her to bring me the pillow off the couch and she came walking into the bedroom with the pillow in her teeth—I cracked up! She's so funny. She can do things like a normal person can do, but she does notice that I do things different and she will try to do them like me. Sometimes I have to hold my arm up in my teeth to reach for something. When she was really small I'd look behind me and see her with her sleeve in her mouth pulling her arm up in the air. And I just laughed. She's fantastic.

I been thinking lately whether or not I want another child. I really, really do want another child but I don't know if I feel like going through the pregnancy part again. Although the pregnancy I had with her was so good, if I have another one it might not be as good and I don't know if I could go through a terrible one. I know I want her to have a sister or brother because I don't want her to be the only child. I don't want her to be really spoiled. I want her to learn how to share with a sister or brother and how to take care of another part of the family.

What about her father?

She sees her father every day. I think that's very important, too, for her and for me and for him. She loves him to death. I'm glad that she loves him like that. I didn't grow up around my father but I don't feel like there's any loss of love between us.

Did coming from a black family have any effect on your disability?

I think that it made it a little better for me because I don't think I was overprotected or put aside. I feel that I was able to do just as much as my sisters and brothers and just as much as most of my friends. If I wanted to survive and be like everybody else I had to prove that I could do all the things that able-bodied people were able to do. And that was things like being in little clubs, going to different places like to concerts, where many times I could have got stomped and knocked down. I've been in situations where I could have really gotten myself hurt, even killed. In the sixties, at the time of the riots, I was right in the middle of some of those things. I was just lucky enough to come through them. At the time I didn't see it as being dangerous. There's a lot of things in my life that I have done or been through that when I look at them now could have been really terrible for me. I've just pulled through. I used to hang around people that ran around in the street all night and all day. I used to run around with people that were involved in drugs and stuff. I never got myself involved with anything that harmed me or anything but yet I was a part of it. When I was growing up I used to do things to prove to myself that I could do it, like smoke cigarettes, and drink a lot, swear a lot. I used to hang around really bad kids. We were out all night and just did everything. But as I grew older I could see that I had to stop doing the things that I was doing if I wanted any kind of a good life. So I just stopped. I think that's about the time I started coming to college.

What is the good life?

I don't know. I don't think I'm really having the good life. To me a good life would be having a good job where I would be able to make enough money to support myself and my daughter and be able to live in a nice house and even a car. I would like to be married and have a husband with a good job. I'd like to finish my education and I'd like to be able to have enough money saved for my daughter to go to college.

Do you have any general ideas about the difference in attitudes toward disability in black communities and white communities?

I don't know. I noticed it a lot more when I was younger. Whenever I was outside or went someplace with my mother or my family or anybody, I could always turn around and know that people were staring at me or talking about me. But in the project where my mother lives now everybody knows me. And I think that I have been kind of good for them because without me being there a lot of these people may not have been exposed to a handicapped person. A lot of them have gotten to know me, and I know their kids. They ask me questions about my disability, and I answer them. So it's something that has helped them, and it's helped me too — being able to listen to little kids laugh and talk about me and ask me questions and wonder what's wrong with my legs, what's wrong with my arms, why do I walk this way? I was at my mother's house one day and my little niece said, "Well, my aunt walks like this," and she started hoppin' like I walk and I thought that was really funny because she noticed me. I could tell that she knew that there was something different. It was something that she saw, she realized, and so it's like a teaching thing.

Do you face similar problems as a black and as a disabled person?

The disabled are really getting together and trying to make sure that things get done. But for me, as long as I have been black I have been aware of blacks trying to band together and help each other, and of blacks losing that battle for a long time. I think when you lose so much it's not as easy to try to get together and start a fight to help yourself. But for disabled people, it's almost as if we're kind of starting off new and if we lose a certain battle it won't be as painful as it would be to blacks that have been fighting for a number of generations and are still going through the same things that they were going through hundreds of years ago, from killings to lynching to the Ku Klux Klan coming in to a certain town. Nothing has changed. The Ku Klux Klan is still there ready to string up a black man or ready to rape a black woman and say someone else did it.

There are a lot of white people that are jealous and just plain hateful towards blacks. I feel they think that blacks might want to get revenge for something that's happened years and years ago, when all it is is that we want an equal share. Like me being disabled, I just want what able-bodied people want, I just want to be able to get in and out of doors. And I want to be able to make as much money as an average white man can make. But if there are a lot of white men that don't even want their wives to be able to make as much money as they do, you can imagine that they really wouldn't want somebody black to be able to make as much money.

Why do you think disabled people can succeed where blacks may not have succeeded?

First of all there are more white disabled people in these groups, fighting and lobbying and protesting for the rights that they want. When they get together and they are out there and they want something, it's not considered a riot. People don't say, send the police down there and be ready to bust their heads, and shit like that. They think, look we're going to have to give these people something because they're making everybody look at them and they're making everybody aware of what they need, so it would be better if we maybe bent their way a little bit.

I don't know why other black people haven't been as involved in organizing—if they don't want to come or if it's because other black disabled people don't know about these things. But there are not enough black disabled people being noticed. I'm sure that there are a greater number of black people who are disabled—in situations like mine—and I think that they should be recognized and I think that they should be involved. We should band together as a group, for jobs and going to schools, to get in and out of doors, in and out of buildings, to be able to go to bathrooms wherever we may be. Until the majority of the world is aware of our difficulties and what we need as individuals, until these things are really heard and looked at, they're not going to be taken care of. We're just like everybody else no matter if we're white, black, women, men, children, grownups, whatever.

I have been trying very hard to get involved in different organizations and different awareness groups. In fact, I'm very interested in writing a book about my life and my disability to let other people know what it's like to be disabled. I have even been thinking about trying to do some kind of a film or something showing how I take care of my daughter because it would give a lot of other disabled people ideas on how to do things as far as taking care of a baby or just doing things for themselves. I think it's good to share ideas because it's really helpful.

How do you see your future?

When I graduate, I would like to have complete rest for one year, and then after that I would like to seek some kind of good paying job. But right now things are very difficult. There was a time when the state rehab department would pay for my tuition and for transportation and for books, but they have discontinued paying for anything but transportation for one year, and I have to maintain a C or better in my grades to get that. Also I have been going through a number of personal problems, emotional and otherwise. A couple of years ago I wouldn't have been able to cope because I wasn't as strong as I am now. But now that I have been seeing a therapist, talking with her, being able to see myself the way I really am, being able to see other people for what they really are, being able to speak up for myself and face problems and deal with certain situations that I couldn't deal with before, I am a lot more mature, and really just a lot stronger, as far as doing things for myself and with other people that I wasn't able to do before. If I do not pass all my courses that I have now, next semester the rehab department will not pay for anything. So, if things don't go right for me this semester in school I will be without funds at all. And next year's supposed to be my last year in school. So, I'm trying very hard.

I don't want to be poor all my life, I don't want to be on welfare. I don't want to be just nobody. I want my daughter to be proud of me and I want to be proud of myself. I want to make a contribution to the world. I want to be able to give other people some kind of knowledge. But even if I never obtain my B.A., I still feel as if I have enough knowledge to give to other people and enough love, and I think that's what the world needs. I think that people should feel free to give each other their knowledge and open to give each other love.

Peter Leech

*I met Pete in his California home. It had ramps to accom-
modate his wheelchair. Crucial devices were set low, well within
his reach. Part of his story is told in the psychotherapeutic
language of his profession. His understanding is set in relief
against the economic, political, and social facts of his life.*

*Pete speaks of having once had the attitudes toward
disability that society at large has. He says that this is where
disabled people start. There is no reason to believe that a member
of a group constructed by society in the first place should be im-
mune from the beliefs that are one manifestation of that construction. Part of Pete's story is a rejection of those beliefs and
learning to define himself on his own terms. This reshaping of
oneself can be used in the face of awkward situations,
discrimination, and a host of other social problems—and con-
stitutes a social recovery from disability.*

*Social recovery is not easy. It may even be incomplete in
many disabled people. But outgrowing the attitudes of society
and forming one's own attitudes is a large part of what gives the
people in these pages the right to view a future when an able-
bodied society has the same beliefs about the disabled that the
people in these pages have about themselves.*

I had polio and became totally physically dependent in 1956
at the age of twenty-three. That was a good many years ago. My
current professional identity is as a licensed clinical social
worker. I have an independent practice in psychotherapy which,
essentially, is a general practice. I do a lot of consulting with

135

hospital nursing staffs and that kind of thing, as well as working with counseling programs, and doing training — especially related to questions and problems of people with physical disabilities.

How did you get from the first to the second?

When the full impact hit me that I was going to be permanently damaged, permanently disabled, I was infused with the same attitudes that people in society at large have about other people who are severely physically disabled. Namely, that I wouldn't be worth anything, nobody would like me, nobody would want to be with me: I'd be a dependent, ineffective, noncontributory and "in-valid" person. I didn't want to be that and the only response I had available at that time was to reject what I thought I had become and say, "No, I don't want to be this." In retrospect I've come to understand that that's where people with disabilities start — having all the attitudes of society at large — and that this contributes in great measure to the rejection of one's self and depression that newly disabled people experience.

It was around that time, say within two to three months after the acute polio, I think, that the only thing that I felt I had left to do that made any sense was to kill myself. I had been able to get out of an iron lung; my diaphragm had begun to work again. I was in bed most of my time, except when I got up in a wheelchair to go to physical therapy, on a rocking bed which aided my breathing. I had an open tracheotomy and the only way I could imagine killing myself might be to choke on a glass of water. But the rocking bed, the open tracheotomy, and the fact that there were people around all the time made it impossible. Nobody would allow that to happen. So there I was, stuck, stewing in my own juices so to speak.

The hospital I was in happened to be on a hill overlooking the tallest building in town, which was the building I had worked in, just out of the service as a photographic lab technician for a railroad. The thing that hit me with such profound impact was that when the bed rocked up I could peek over the windowsill and see down the hill. I could see the elevators going up and down in that building. One day it hit me: Good grief the world is still going on out there! How could that possibly be when this kind of a thing has happened? This is a major catastrophe — How come people are still driving around and going to work doing their thing?

I had the GI Bill available to me for going to college. I had thought a bit about going to college after I got out of the service and thought I'd work for awhile and get things together. Now I began to realize that the only way I could make any money was to go to college. So that's what I did. It was a purely economic decision at that point because I still had the built-in sense that I had to figure out some way to support myself. The only thing I could figure, the *only* thing, was to go to college.

I had vocational counseling and stuff like that, and they told me my best possibility was to learn to become an accountant. That idea just really put me off. I thought, God, I couldn't possibly do anything like that with my life; it's not me — I need some other kind of contact with people; math has always been one of my weakest points; I just couldn't do that. And I told them that. It was tantamount to what I've come to call agency or institutional suicide. You say something like that to a rehabilitation counselor — somebody who's got all those good intentions and has come up with the best thing for you to do and you reject that — they say, "Well there's nothing I can do for you" (which is totally unreasonable). "We feel we just can't work with him."

Well, luckily I had the GI Bill and I could go to college. I had had an interest in medicine. I took a couple of summer courses and did okay and decided if nothing else I could at least try out the pre-medical curriculum and see what happened. I began to do that and at the same time I was hoping for more strength to develop in my upper extremities and hands, as well as looking forward to reconstructive hand surgery. I also had met a fellow who was in his third year of medical school when I was in the hospital who was a post-polio paraplegic. He became my first role model among people who had severe disabilities who were functioning effectively.

How important do you think role models are?

I think they're incredibly important. One thing that's most lacking in the lives of people with physical disabilities, whether they're infants or children or adults, is role models among other people with severe disabilities who are functioning effectively. The isolation, and the way families and schools and teachers and other agencies try to keep that from happening, is really tragic. It may be one of my heretical ideas about counseling and working with people with disabilities. I think that one of our greatest needs is contact with other people with disabilities for reasons that I'll get to later. So anyway, with that kind of stimulation I thought, Okay, I'll try premed, and see what happens.

I spent two and a half years in premed. During that time I went through the hand surgery and realized that I wasn't going to get all the upper extremity and hand function I wanted, and was working slowly in labs. Finally in organic chemistry—which was said to be one of the pulling out points of premedical students—I was having a lot of trouble, enough trouble with theory but a terrible time with labs because there's just too much moving around to do. I asked for extra labs and they told me that it would be unfair to the other students to allow me to have extra labs. But I think probably something else was going on. My suspicion is that they maybe realized that if I were working that slowly (and this is the thing I finally told myself), even if I got into medical school I'd not be able to work quickly enough to get through. Maybe I could have developed a specialty in medicine that would have been fine but, anyway, that's what I finally told myself and I suspect that even if they weren't consciously aware of it, people had some sense of that.

It's not very different from all the hassle I had to go through to get my language requirement. The German Department at my university was on the third floor of a building which had maybe fifteen or twenty stairs up to the first floor, and no elevator once you got inside. German was offered on the third floor, and they would not change that class around to an accessible building for me because, they told me, they don't do that for individual students, they just don't do that! So, I had to make arrangements to get to that third floor five days a week for the three quarters that I took German—rain or snow, ice or sunshine. I had at least three fellows who helped out a lot, all of whom were mountain climbers, any one of whom could give me a hand independently up all those stairs and give me a hand back down again. I am eternally grateful for their energy, their time, and their faith that I was going to do something with the opportunity once I got there.

Here's another example of the same kind of hassle. When I

initially applied, they told me they wouldn't let me into the university because I was disabled and didn't believe I could get through, and that they just don't have physically disabled students on this campus. It was my state university, and when I'd applied three years before—after working a couple of years after high school and thinking that going to college might be a good idea after all—they had told me that I didn't have good enough grades to go to school there—that if I went to a private college and got good grades, or was a veteran, then they'd have to let me in, even on probation. Well, I went to a local college for one quarter before I went into the service, and got good grades, and now I was a veteran, and they were telling me I couldn't be admitted! I was very angry, I really made a fuss. I know in retrospect that it wasn't for the right reasons. I was making a fuss because they were going back on their word, not because they were being prejudicial and actively discriminating against me because I was physically disabled.

And you really have reason to believe that they were actively discriminating?

Oh, sure. I was told that directly. "You can't go to school here because we never had a 'wheelchair patient' go to school here." I was angered because they were going back on their word they'd given me years before. So I made a fuss and finally got somebody in a suit and tie who came out and said, "What's all the fuss about." And I said, "You're the person I want to talk to, and this is my problem." The person said, "Well, we ought to try it." And they did.

Anyway, when I decided to change out of the premedical curriculum I told myself that I probably ought to pick something at which I could excel without killing myself, and the first thing that presented itself was another dilemma—an economic dilemma. Under the GI Bill you have to get a degree within a certain amount of time or lose your benefits. So I looked around and decided that I could get a degree in sociology within the next two quarters if I took the right courses. So I did and I got a B.A. in sociology. I recognized that as a dead end also because when I started looking around at what kind of jobs I could get a hold of (I'm again thinking only of economics, trying to develop my own way of becoming economically independent), I saw it would mean working for the State Department of Employment or the Welfare Department or something like that—relatively low level, without any power, without being able to move to a higher level—and I thought of that as a dead end, partly because I was beginning to feel as though I had more to offer than that. So I began to think about a way to study psychology, and discovered that it would take five years for me to get a graduate degree that would make me employable, give me a skill I could market. In contrast, I could get a graduate degree in social work in two years—so again, I chose the expedient course of action!

I applied to the University of California at Berkeley in 1961 and entered into a lengthy correspondence with the graduate division. In the first letter I confessed that I had a physical disability. They sent back a letter giving me all the reasons why I very likely would not be able to make it on their campus. I responded to every one of their points with another letter, saying that I didn't get sick all the time, that I had made it around the university at a place with very harsh winters, which must be more difficult than U.C. Berkeley—at least there wouldn't be a lot of snow and ice on the ground during a lot of the winter—that I did make good grades, and that the one place I had screwed up was when I had taken withdrawals from organic chemistry, physics, and college algebra at a time in the quarter when I couldn't get a passing withdrawal. Three pages later I gave them the names of professors to contact, physicians to contact, all sorts of stuff. I got back a very terse note saying, "Besides, your grades aren't high enough." I then applied to the University of Illinois for grad school in social work, only to be told that the only program not accessible to physically disabled students was the Graduate School of Social Work. It was in a building off campus upstairs in an old house and there was just no way to do it; they were very sorry but that was it.

The sense I had of it then and retain now was that the University of California's rejection was discriminatory. But I knew that the University of Illinois had made every effort to make it possible for students to get around the campus and that this particular program was just a happenstance thing that it wasn't possible to deal with. It was the only program there, I believe, that a physically disabled student couldn't participate in.

I felt okay about that. It wasn't actively discriminatory. They even gave me an indication that within a year they would be transferring into another building, which would be accessible if I wanted to apply then.

The University of Washington also has a graduate school of social work and that's where I ended up going. They had an accessible building; they also had one instructor who was severely physically disabled from polio. I turned out to have a marvelous experience with him, partly because he had done his own rehabilitation work at Georgia Warm Springs at the same time as Franklin Roosevelt, and so had a lot of deep background to share about the whole thing: disability, Roosevelt, politics, and social programs.

I believe that Roosevelt saw his disability as a weakness that he would prefer to hide and avoid as much as possible, except where it was politically opportune for him to reveal it. In most of the things he did in national politics (this is really an off-the-top of my head reaction) he tried to appear as physically able as possible. There are some people even now who never knew that he had a physical disability—that he had no use of his lower extremities whatsoever. He always appeared standing behind a podium. In photographs with other statesmen he was sitting down on a couch or something like that. There's one little-known story about him going down for the inaugural for the governorship of New York. He always had these heavy duty guys—bodyguard types—who were incredibly strong and would function as his attendants and helpers in all kinds of ways. He walked down the aisle on his braces, but without crutches or anything, as if he was just walking along. There was always one guy in front of him who paid careful attention to the ground and kicked cigarette butts, pebbles, and stuff like that out of the way so he wouldn't trip or fall. But he missed something, and one of Roosevelt's feet hit it and he lost his balance completely. But the guys alongside of him just held their arms out and he supported all his weight on their arms while they continued down the hall without breaking their stride. They went for about thirty feet trying to get him into some kind of striding before he managed to get his feet back underneath him, and nobody ever knew that he was being carried for that period of time. Other times he would go up fire escapes at the backsides of buildings to appear at upper floor conference rooms and luncheons. He would just appear and stand behind the podium to speak, so he wouldn't be seen coming up the front stairs and having to have help.

He, I think, could have been *the* role model for somebody who had had polio—could have done a much greater service for people with disabilities even back then. But he was politically astute also, and may have realized that it would have been political death for him to be more up front about that whole thing, even if he was personally able to manage it. I have some reason to believe that personally he managed it fairly well. He was driving a car with hand controls before anyone else imagined anything like that. I think it was a Model T outfitted with hand controls. But hiding his disability was, I think, a disservice to people with disabilities; I think people with disabilities could have gotten a big boost, could have been further ahead now had Roosevelt been willing to lead the disabled movement in the 1930s.

Anyway, back to my career. I decided to go into the Graduate School of Social Work because by then I'd begun to be able to see a place where I could focus and begin to be useful. A lot of it began to flow out of my own intuition and my own awareness that things were happening with me emotionally that nobody else had been able to help me with.

Have you ever had psychotherapy?

I had a year (aside from talking with a social worker and other people while I was in the hospital) after I started going to school. I was feeling very depressed and very out of place, feeling that I didn't have friends who considered me a contributing member within the friendship. I went to the student health center and saw a psychiatrist. For whatever reason—whether it was because I didn't have sense enough to ask the right things, or his therapeutic style—he never gave back to me that what was going on within me had to do in great measure with the fact that I was newly disabled. My depression, my feeling I was out of sorts, out of place, unable to focus on things, had to do primarily with the fact that I'd become disabled. But he didn't even use that language. I don't know what was going on behind that rather bland facade but we didn't confront it and I think he could have helped me immeasurably if he had confronted it with me, if he'd been able to share his own fears, if he'd been able to really get into it and say, Look, tell me about this, I don't know anything about physical disabilities, I don't know what's going on with you, but something's got to be going on.

How would you, as a therapist, have dealt with yourself?

By way of history I would have heard that it was only a year ago that I had contracted polio, and I would have asked direct questions. How has that affected your life? Tell me what's changed, what about the way you see yourself? How *do* you see yourself? Do you have dreams? How do you see yourself in your dreams? What does it feel like when you wake up from a dream seeing yourself that way? What does it mean when you compare that image in the dream with the image of yourself now, sitting in a wheelchair?

See, I had had a series of recurrent dreams over a relatively long time span. The first one occurred when I was still hospitalized and I must have been five or six months into my disability. At that time, I was still lying back in a reclining wheelchair, I wasn't able to push myself, wasn't able to get around independently at all. I was beginning to be able to feed myself independently and do some minimal activities, like hold a pencil and a fork strapped to my fingers, use arm slings with a razor strapped to my hand to begin to try to shave myself and wash myself. The first dream, while I was still in the hospital, awakened me in a really heavy anxiety. It was a very simple dream. The dream setting was the hospital corridor and I'm kind of like eyes in the wall looking out at the hospital corridor. Someone with my name is walking down the corridor and going from my right down to my left. I'm at the extreme end of one of the hospital corridors, watching. People, heads of people on the staff are popping out of doorways just after he passes and they're saying, "Wow, look at him, isn't he tall and doesn't he walk well. My goodness, I've never seen the like of that, isn't that wonderful, that's marvelous!" I woke up out of a dead sleep in a cold sweat, freaked out at this dream. Full recollection of the dream but no connection... I just couldn't understand what was going on, it had shaken me so. That was about three a.m. I thought about it and thought about it and kind of brooded over it. By the afternoon of that day it finally hit me.

My God! The disparity between that person with my name and the me that was here in this wheelchair was so profound that the impact was just incredible.

Over the next two years this same dream recurred a number of different times, I can't remember exactly how many of these there were. The next one was the same scene, same setting, same people poking out, same words, but the person with my name is walking down the hall with a limp. The next one is him walking down the hall with a limp and a cane, I guess. Then one of him walking very well with long leg braces and crutches. Next he's struggling on long leg crutches and has a pelvic band but is still walking. Through that to one where he is really whistling along in a wheelchair, then he is getting along in a wheelchair but not quite so great. I guess the last in that series, and the way I see myself now in my dreams, is where he is sitting down using a wheelchair getting around a little better than I can — getting up over a five or six inch curb without any wheelchair limitations for instance. I could see that reality and the image I had of myself were gradually pulling together so that I began to feel more of a whole.

You were talking about the way that you would have treated yourself.

I'm simply not afraid to confront those things any more because of what I've been through — up to and including having the experience of my own dying. I was fully conscious, I was aware a great deal of the time when I was so deeply ill. Even when they were saying, "He's not responding, he probably can't hear you," I knew my father was there. Because of that I work pretty well with people who are dying. I'm sure there are lots of things I need to learn, but I'm not afraid of death, not afraid to talk to people about it, not afraid to be there with them. Nor am I afraid to talk to people about their disabilities and their pain, their anger, their sadness, what they've lost, and all those kinds of things. I think that's a unique training experience that very few professionals have or are able to get. I'm able to move into it and confront it, where the usual method is to deny it — to suggest that people not think about it, don't cry, it's better if you don't cry, you'll feel better tomorrow, don't be angry, I didn't do this, I'm trying to help you, you shouldn't be angry with me. My opinion is that those things need to be expressed. I know I needed it because it wasn't until many years later that I finally got into a therapeutic experience that would encourage me to move that way, and intuitively I believe that it makes sense. Your telling me I shouldn't be angry doesn't make any sense. But it took getting into the experience and really going with it to validate what I'd known intuitively all along. I now feel very strongly that that's the right way to go. So when I start working with anybody who's had any kind of loss, rather than try to patch up that facade and stiffen up that upper lip and dry the tears, I move into it in the other direction and say, "Well, there's lots that must be going on and I want to hear about all of it."

This is life after all, the nitty gritty of what's going on. And if it happens to carry with it all the emotions that we usually assign to the negative side of the ledger—the sadness, the anger, the sorrow and all those kinds of things—then they must be allowed to live, just as much as the happiness and the joy and the caring and all the rest of it. If all my energy is tied up in not looking at the painful things or the losses I've experienced or the anger, then my energy is not available for me to do the things I need to do. If I work at not looking at something that's going on with me I tend to emphasize it also because it becomes something I'm *not looking at now*: "I'm not going to look at this anymore. No, I really must not look at it." Once I tap into it and say, Okay, I'm looking at these things, then it's done and the energy is released. You get through to the energy that is there and you have the energy to go on.

What do you have against denial?

Denial has all kinds of meanings attached to it. If you have a connection with something and you lose it, you're going to experience sadness. One can get into a situation of denying that anything was lost and you've probably been familiar with people who are stuck in that state of being. A person was hit by a truck, sustained a serious cord injury, after three months he's still in a circle bed and he's talking as if next week he's going to be out playing football again, or going hiking. Cold denial is one stage in a state of being. First there's shock. That very quickly gives way to an experience of hurt and, very likely, anger. It's as if all the stuff you've been told all your life wasn't true. Now you're supposed to forget it. The job doesn't matter, a family doesn't matter. So you deny the experience. The state of denial, I think, is an avoidance of the experience of loss, and very often one of the ways that that experience is manifested is in tears. What happens within medical settings usually is that if a person begins to cry they're told not to cry. If they continue to cry then somebody's called to fix it—psychiatrists, social workers, medical doctors to administer medication—to keep the tears away. I think that functions to keep the experience of sadness away, which tends to keep the experience of loss away, which tends to support, encourage, consolidate and crystallize denial as a state of being and people get stuck there.

The able-bodied can get stuck in that state of being, too. They're denying something at another level. I suspect that they tend to deny their own vulnerability. I think people would much rather pretend that they don't have anything to worry about. People get into automobiles everyday, drive down the street, and probably don't use their seatbelts and shoulder harness. There has to be a good deal of denial that goes into that activity, to take a really simple example—denial of the fact that over 65,000 people each year get killed doing that very same thing, and I don't know how many thousands suffer injuries as a result: brain injuries, physical disabilities, or whatever. I don't think people want to get in touch with the fact that they're vulnerable that way; and if they see me crying that puts them in touch with it. They'd rather say, "Stop that."

What about children with disabilities and their families?

The family of an infant who is disabled from birth, who goes through the system of care for disabled kids, goes through school for handicapped kids, and who has normal intellectual ability, retains attitudes that have the same historical roots as the family of a young man who gets on his motorcycle and rides off to school one day and breaks his neck in an accident. The young man who rode off in his motorcycle and suffered a cervical cord injury and the kid who's disabled from birth end up at a comparable place emotionally unless something remarkable happens in the family of the kid who's been disabled from birth. That place is a situation where the family would prefer to deny that it ever happened; it's too painful, they don't want to get in touch with their own vulnerabilities, they don't know what to do. It's a pain in the ass that they don't want to have to confront because that would mean being angry that it happened, and how could you be angry at a kid who's had an accident or a kid who's been born with a disability. This, of course, is nonsense. Of course you can be angry at the event, or the attitudes but they pretend that you can't be angry because if you're going to be angry you have to be angry at *someone* and that's not allowable. So they retain all the attitudes about the poor disabled person who is invalid, asexual, ineffective, noncontributory forever. Even the kid who is born with the disability is going to end up feeling really out of sorts, feeling like she or he just doesn't belong — not getting many breaks in regard to being independent and effective and contributory and those kinds of things — and having folks that will go along with the system, you know: "They'll never be able to get anywhere and do anything so this school is just fine; this workshop is just fine. Oh, the future? Don't think about the future right now, today is another school day." So the child ends up with a sense-of-self that doesn't fully incorporate the damaged body and is therefore disparate, and disunified. And there's a feeling that "I wish I didn't have to look at anything below my eyes, because if I do that I have to recognize that parts of me don't quite work right or look right."

Could I change the subject for a minute and ask you to briefly describe a few case histories and the contributions you were able to make as a therapist who is himself disabled?

Sure. Let's see. All right, very briefly. Let me tell you about a situation that pops into mind right now. I was asked to see a fourteen-year-old girl because she was hallucinating — that was what was focused on as the presenting problem, fearful hallucinations, auditory and visual. She lived in a family with an older sister and two parents, all successful, vibrant dynamic people. She had a stroke when she was young and she had some residual paralysis. So I see her and find that a recurrent thing happens whenever she starts to get together or has been together with friends her own age, and the evening comes on and she's home. She hears the voice of a little girl laughing at her and sees occasional flips of the appearance of this girl. So I ask her, what does she look like? "Well, she looks remarkably like me." Oh, can you explain that any further? "She seems like she's about eleven, that big, with blond hair." And so on. She presents a fairly clear cut picture of herself laughing.

Well, how do I work with that? First, I ask about the hallucination she hears. What does it sound like, what do you hear from it, what do you get out of it, what words do you get out of it, what feelings does it give you? "It doesn't give any feelings." Can you just reproduce for me what it sounds like? And eventually we work back to the girl owning the voice and the laugh and all the feelings that go along with it. Her hallucinations clear up when she begins to confront all the feelings she's had about being disabled—especially now that she's entered puberty and wants to start to date and has a lot of feelings about boys, especially about boys not liking her—that whole thing. She's in a family structure that's very supportive, but trying to move her toward independence without ever confronting all the worries she must have about that. The parents had really been hurt deeply. The big, strong, vibrant father came in, a very successful guy, and within five minutes crumbled into tears in my office after years of holding it all back—saying just how much he was hurt by the whole thing, how much it continues to hurt to have to see her struggle all the time. I said, "Dammit, she has to struggle or else she's not going to live. How can you help her with that?" And so they all began to get it together and began to work as a unit towards understanding what the girl is experiencing, rather than saying don't think about that, don't listen to it, don't worry about that; or you shouldn't be so sad, it'll all pass, someday you'll feel better. The result was the girl didn't need the hallucinations any longer and the family could all work together on the real challenges.

I can think of another case—a young man who had cerebral palsy. He had an older brother who had no difficulties and parents who preferred not to be concerned with him. The father was a successful dentist, had all kinds of money and was able to live a really good life. The kid had a great deal of drive, interest in living. I got the referral from the physically disabled students' program. They referred him as a young man who was depressed—no, not even depressed—a young man who needed to get some help with an emotional problem before the department of rehabilitation would help him. I said, "Okay, sounds like somebody I should see, have him call me." So he called me—he had some speech difficulty but not beyond comprehension on the telephone—and we worked out an appointment. I give people a choice about whether they come up the driveway and use the ramp or come in through the other gate and go along a cobblestone walk. I asked him and he said he walked. He appeared in my office, able to walk, very strong, with considerable arm function but with a certain amount of intention tremor. I asked him what was going on. Well, he had just come back to the University after being out for awhile. He wanted to get the department of rehabilitation to help him out with tuition, but they wouldn't because of his emotional problems. So I asked him what his emotional problems were and he said, "Well, I'm feeling pretty good right now, but I've been depressed and I also feel that I don't have any friends, feel embarrassed in public and stuff like that." In particular he was embarrassed about his speech. I thought he had had this for a long time, but upon exploration, it turned out he hadn't! He had had some surgery about two years previously that was supposed to resolve his tremor, but what it did was create more difficulties: he began having trouble walking, and it screwed up his speech. Here we've got a guy who's not only been disabled from birth, but is also a *newly* disabled adult! I wouldn't have found this out, if I hadn't been willing to talk about his disability in detail, and the ways it was affecting his life.

I gather you think it important that people who deliver services to the disabled also be disabled. Why?

I believe that they should comprehend the disabled experience—and people with disabilities are more likely to grasp this. It's primarily so that the kind of needs that people with disabilities have can be more directly satisfied. Too often the usual professional approach is to get some training and/or experience in a particular thing, and maybe set up an agency that will provide that kind of thing without it having any relationship at all to what the recipient of the service needs, really. It maintains a kind of superior-inferior relationship between the provider of service and the recipient of service; it also ignores what the recipient of the service really needs.

Let's take the medical model. The medical model for the provision of services starts out with the definition of the physician-patient relationship: the physician is the individual who knows all about medicine and other things, and the patient is a person who is in dire need of the physician's service. It starts out with the physician knowing everything, and the patient knowing nothing other than that he or she hurts or is in some other kind of medical emergency. The patient looks to the physician to define not only the problem, but to provide services to resolve the immediate emergency. Unfortunately, one of the things that happens within the disabled experience is that once you're a patient you're always seen as a patient. Anyone who sits down in a wheelchair and appears out in public, for instance, immediately sets up the response in the imagination of the viewer that that person is somehow a "patient," probably invalid, those kinds of things, and, therefore, has to be always the dependent recipient of the services of everybody else around them — including physicians, nurses, physical therapists, occupational therapists, welfare workers, teachers, people on the street, on down the line.

There is a clear confusion in this country between disability and illness, so that seeing a person that has a residual disability sets up in the viewer the sense that the person is also ill, and if you're ill you're then a patient. This pervasive confusion, I think, has an historical base. Over the last three thousand years, say, man, genus *Homo*, has been superior in intelligence and ability to the rest of the animal world in developing ways of managing his environment, but also pretty inferior in terms of strength and stamina. It's been very clear over this whole history that, given that a human being becomes injured in a way that's going to slow him down even more than he ever was, he's going to immediately be dependent, probably vulnerable, and not last very long. That's a historical tradition that goes way, way back. I don't think that the history of merely the last thirty to forty years, within which people who've been injured or seriously ill have been enabled by medical technology to recover (even though they may have a residual disability), is going to erase all the assumptions set up by that historical tradition. So the gut reaction to somebody with a disability is that that person is vulnerable, weak, probably ill, and won't last very long in this world. That tradition has a very long foundation and needs to be confronted now in the light of recent medical technology — *very* recent in our historical framework.

If I were to rely only on my training and professional experience I probably would be stuck in that tradition also. The advantage to me of being physically disabled and also developing a profession and education and experience has been that I've had the ability to view things from both sides of the fence. Coming out of a situation of total physical dependence after having had polio, and having a chance to experience in its fullest the actual situation of being totally physically dependent on physicians, nurses, and the rest, I became aware of how the system sets up the situation of permanent dependence, and realized that unless I fought my way out of it, the system would render me permanently dependent. I've had the chance to modify the attitudinal set that professional education, professional experience, and agency policies maintain. And I have had a chance to modify it in the agencies I've worked in and also to modify my whole approach to the question of counseling and providing service to people with disabilities.

What do you mean by "the system"?

The internal politics of any agency define that agency as all-knowing and omnipotent. Since the individual is dependent on the agency for assistance, the system sees the individual, then, as totally dependent. His/her need may differ from what the agency provides. The individual could possibly help the agency define more clearly what services are needed, but the agencies, because they're superior and the recipient is inferior, are able to say, "Those just aren't possible. We don't have them. You're out of luck." That's the kind of system that tends to maintain the dependence of anybody who's been down. That person may very clearly be physically dependent, but the system also assumes they're emotionally dependent — can't begin to assume intellectual control of their own lives again, so their own definition of their need holds no credence.

Let's use the example of a person with severe physical disability being able to live and function in an independent living situation, that is, a situation that is independent of his own family and independent of another care institution. Several states now have what is called an attendant care program that provides money to hire people to perform the physical services that a person who is severely physically disabled needs in order to get ready for life—getting up in the morning, getting washed, getting dressed, taking care of bowel and bladder functions, getting into the wheelchair, and having the attendant fix (and possibly help someone to eat) breakfast. That person may then very well go out and put in a full day's work at some kind of activity (going to school or to a job). The physical services provided by an attendant are a necessary part of the severely disabled individual's life. Given a way to pay somebody to do that kind of thing, a person with a severe physical disability can live independently of a convalescent home or family situation and manage an independent life. The attendant care program makes it possible for money to be paid directly to severely disabled persons, who can then hire, pay, train, and fire, if necessary, their own attendants.

Now, there are other ways of providing that care: California and the federal law also provide for what's called homemaker services, where people are trained by other agencies to provide attendant care services for persons who have severe physical disabilities. In this kind of program the money (say, $300) goes to an agency providing home care services and that agency then sends somebody out to the person's house. The severely disabled individual has not hired that person, however, or trained that person, so a whole different kind of relationship is set up. Also, a large part of the money goes to providing the administrative costs of the homemaker service program rather than to buying the services of the attendant so that fewer hours of assistance are available. In addition, service agencies often do not provide anybody after five o'clock in the afternoon or before nine o'clock in the morning or on weekends. So, here again is the problem of a system that maintains dependency.

Living independently is the simple matter of having control over how your life is going to work. On the one hand, assume the position of a person with a severe disability who calls up an agency and says, "I need someone to give me a hand with my physical needs." They say, "We can only do that between nine and five o'clock on weekdays." Consider the difference in gut level experience and independence between that situation and the one where the individual is given the money directly, so that he or she can call somebody at nine o'clock at night and say, "I need you to come over right now and since you're my employee I expect you do that," or get someone to come on weekends so the individual can go out to a play or film or something like that. I think the profound sense of dependence that people with severe disabilities get into begins to lift given that kind of service. It's a matter of giving a person the wherewithal to take more control over his or her own life and that has a lot of psychological impact, just as it has psychological impact with a two-year-old child who's begun to do something differently and has begun to be able to be more independent.

Let me check out what you mean by independent.

The kind of independence that I talk about has as its focal point the degree of control that the individual is willing and able to assume over his or her own life, given that the person is physically dependent in certain ways, as I am. I'm physically dependent on a wheelchair, I'm physically dependent on an automobile that I can manage to get my wheelchair into and out of and drive with hand controls. I'm physically dependent on parking being available near a place where I need to go or on curb ramps being installed. If those things didn't exist I would be physically dependent on another person in some form—either somebody I know who is going with me to a place, or somebody off the street who I ask to give me a hand up over the curb. I'm physically dependent in those ways, yet I'm still defining *where* I want to go, *when* I want to go there, *how* I want to get there. In that way, I'm independent.

Let's say that a hundred years from now we've managed to get those ideas pretty well across; let's say the general public is fairly well informed about physical disability and the attitudes and stereotypes that have been with us for thousands of years are minimized. I still may want to go downtown at a time when there may not be a lot of other people around, so I get in my car and I drive downtown. I get out of my car, and there I am—on a curb, wanting to go across the street, and there's no one around. In that situation I would prefer to have curb ramps so I can go down the curbs, across the street and up the curb on the other side without waiting for somebody to come along. Imagine a world that would be workable independently. It wouldn't have to be designed specifically for people with physical disabilities. The things that exist as architectural barriers to people with severe disabilities are also architectural barriers to another large segment of the population. We've worked medical technology well enough to develop a large physically disabled population; we're also going to have an older and older population. As people age they may become less able to climb stairs or drag their market baskets up over curbs. They may want to give up their private automobiles because they don't feel competent as drivers anymore, but may not be able to climb the stairs on the public transportation buses and that kind of thing. The older a person becomes, the more difficult it is for them to get onto a bus or streetcar. The technology exists to make sidewalks, buses, and streetcars accessible; it simply hasn't been employed. The population of aged people, which is going to become larger and larger, would benefit from it, not to mention younger people with market baskets or babies in strollers.

Let me give it to you directly: Why should a taxpayer want to pay enough money for curb ramps, pay the money that's required for attendant care service? All these things cost money.

There are two reasons. The first, I think, is a moral issue. Society, the taxpayers if you will, has given the medical profession sanction to keep babies alive who have severe physical problems — to get them through the first months of life when they might have expired had it not been for the good medical treatment and that kind of thing. It's also given the medical profession sanction to keep people alive through devastating injuries and illnesses. Given that society sanctions that, I don't think it's morally right to keep those infants, those children and developing adults, and those adults or older people who have been disabled by injury or illness alive simply as lab experiments. I don't think man was intended to exist as a lab experiment, kept alive behind glass doors. There's a moral responsibility to allow those who've been kept alive to develop as much functional independence as possible. And we have the technology to do it — not only the medical technology to keep people alive, but the technology to make it possible for people with severe physical problems to function at a high level of independence.

Look at the population statistics. There are huge numbers of men missing from the populations of Germany and Russia and France and the United States as a result of the First World War. Huge populations missing of young men who went off to war, were injured to one degree or another, and didn't survive. The Second World War, with all its broader range and more devastating fire power, did not create quite as large a gap of missing people (at least from the United States' population) primarily because those men could be kept alive. That kind of thing, in and of itself, has created a larger population with disabilities. It's growing and growing all the time. That's one pressure that we see—medical technology that's developed incredibly. Along with that, the technology has been developed to make people more functional—just amazing use of machinery, electrical devices. For example, the electrified wheelchair, a relatively simple device, has made it possible for a person who's totally paralyzed to get around town independently. That's one simple part of it. Then there are all kinds of other assistive devices, electric motors, switches and fans, and all kinds of things.

How come the taxpayer would want to support all this? Aside from the moral issue, there's a simple monetary issue. Take a person who's been severely disabled and is kept alive and sent back home again, say to live with his family. Families can take care of a person for a certain period of time, but families die away. They get old and they can't manage anymore. What's happened in the past is that persons with severe disabilities get relegated to convalescent hospitals. One man I worked closely with spent six years in a county hospital, just being there. Well, that costs a hell of a lot of money. Even in a convalescent hospital (where care and services are minimized) rather than a heavy hospital situation, it must cost around twelve hundred dollars a month to maintain a person. The top amount for attendant care for a person who requires more than thirty-five hours a week is, say, four hundred and fifty dollars a month. That's a third of nursing home care cost, not to mention the opportunities to develop skills, get training of one sort or another, and become economically independent again. People don't like to be economically dependent any more than they like to be physically dependent or dependent in any other way. Maybe you have to support people for 10 years, give them training, maybe a college degree, maybe a graduate degree, supporting them through extra training with extra attendant care. If they then manage to hit a salary level that will allow them to become completely independent economically, it's a lot cheaper economically than supporting them in convalescent hospitals for the rest of their lives. Not to mention the fact that people who are active and have an investment in life again learn how to take care of themselves and don't have as many secondary illnesses—don't have as many ulcers, bladder infections, chest infections—so they aren't going back and using high-cost, acute hospital facilities. Acute hospitalization can cost three hundred dollars a day—the cost of dependency that most taxpayers never hear about!

There's another side of it. People who are encouraged and assisted to become independent, become taxpayers again. I've been disabled for eighteen years, and I've been working in my profession for eleven and a half. I pay as many taxes as any other person. Some of the stuff that my tax monies have paid for I can't use because it's built in a manner that is inaccessible. I think that situation, in particular, is really outrageous. And, as a taxpayer, I have another bone to pick. I know that it's possible to reduce the tax load by spending a little more money initially to get people with severe disabilities back into being independent again, including being economically independent. But the system is using my tax monies and everybody else's to maintain dependence, which is only going to cost more in the long run. I understand that side of the picture also.

I happen to have an investment in life. As I look back, there was a point when I was very near death where I might have chosen differently, especially after awakening to the realization that I was going to be permanently disabled. I have had a lot of thoughts about what the point was of keeping me alive and all that. Yet looking back now, I feel—grateful isn't the quite the word—I feel that it's something going on in the back of people's heads that acknowledges that, even though physically limited, a human being still has potential and can go on and accomplish something. Homo sapiens is a very interesting animal. Even where there's no medical technology, individuals pull together whatever magical resources they can to try to get things to be better, to try and have people recover from illnesses or from disabilities. Once done, I believe that it's the worst use of the tax monies *and* the human potential to maintain a system which fosters dependence.

Doe West

I got to Doe's apartment on Saturday morning. It was on the second floor. The doorbell was broken, so I shouted up. Doe came down to open the door. Her mouth, her face, her body, all one big laugh. She and her manfriend were cleaning up the vestiges of a cream pie fight from the night before. She prided herself on her aim.

Doe had learned to laugh, not a glued on smile but a laugh that came from the belly. It turned out that she was in severe pain as we talked. It may be that laughter in the psychoanalytic sense of that word is a defense against pain. But then defenses may not always be bad. Or, it may be that Doe had learned something.

Doe's handicap is interesting if not fascinating. It's not one of your dependable constant handicaps but swings from vigorous able body to wheelchair body in pain. Doe's body and the relationship of it to the social and physical world can never be taken for granted. As such Doe's reflections on her body as she lives it are illuminating for the different bodies of many handicapped people. For Doe experiences a handicapped body from inside while in a wheelchair and from the outside yet close, tied to memory and anticipation when able-bodied.

Doe's narrative is testimony to the centrality of the body to a handicapped person, and, indeed, of its centrality to the experience of everyone, disabled or able-bodied. Not being able to take her body for granted, Doe asked questions and gave answers about it that begin to reveal what so many of us with constant bodies, similar bodies, bodies around which the able-bodied life is structured, rarely have occasion to question or answer. And yet those questions could well be ours: Do we inhabit our bodies? Do

159

we live with them? Do we own them? Are we our bodies? What is the relationship of our bodies to the structure of society and to the architecture, transportation, organization of work and the rest of our lives?

While predicated on biology, who does and who does not have a handicap and what is to be called a handicap is not biological fact but social artifact. It is this artifact of social construction which is decisive in the lives of handicapped people. Like blacks, women, homosexuals, and others who are different from society's expectation, the handicapped are proclaiming their independence, their self definition, their emancipation, their liberation. To do so means in part to organize together. Organizing together, however, presents a direct problem to people with disabilities. For while disability or handicap may seem monolithic to the vision of an able-bodied world, in fact and to the handicapped person, it is anything but monolithic. Indeed, frequently one handicapped person will share with another primarily the fact of social oppression.

People are handicapped because of the social construction of their "lived bodies," the way their bodies insert themselves into the world, the way they are experienced by society and behave in it. But in fact there are many kinds of lived bodies, all "handicapped" or "disabled." Each sort of body has its own attending problems and pleasures. The blind person cannot see, the deaf person cannot hear, the paraplegic gets from place to place not by walking but by wheeling. And so it goes down a long and complex and interesting list. One person I talked with put it like this: "A while ago pride was something I talked about with a lot of different disabled people. And I didn't get much support for it. Most people said I was crazy and just sort of looked at me. But it really was important to me that we develop a pride in ourselves, just like "black pride" and "sisterhood is powerful" and that we really appreciate what we learn from being disabled. Personally I find that the disabled are somehow a lot more real. They're more interesting to me. I like being with a group of disabled people for a long time, just watching all the different ways their bodies work. And usually after I do that for a day or two at a conference or something, when I go back out into the rest of the world and see all these able-bodied people whose bodies all work the same way somehow it seems boring. You see, there's no difference, no uniqueness."

How would you describe yourself?
As a woman who is in the outer stages of a very intense metamorphosis; somebody who had to go through a second stage of being in order to be the person that she is today. And this revolves around my disability. The person that I was before I became disabled is far different from the person that I am today, and it would seem everybody and everything else seems to have changed around me as well. Obviously, it is just my perception of them that is changed. So, too, it is probably just my perception of my self that has changed. Basic similarities, yet different outgrowths. Sort of my sister self.

When did you become disabled?
About five years ago when I was in junior college. I was pre-med biology. It started out as a stiff knee and within six months it became such generalized pain and stiffness, fever and weakness, that I became wheelchair active and I was in the wheelchair for three years. About a year ago I went into a partial remission. The pain didn't stop, the fevers didn't stop, but a lot of the actual stiffness and inability to move the joints eased off, so I'm parttime wheelchair. In that sense I live in both worlds because this morning I'm "able-bodied" to the world, but this afternoon I may be back in my chair. It's that kind of a yo-yo syndrome.

Do you have any way of knowing when you're going to be disabled or when you're going to be all right?
Absolutely none. I can make an appointment or the arrangements to go to a conference or out on a date and I don't know whether I'm going to do it walking or in the chair. Right now, the remission is slipping, so I've had to go through the readjustment of knowing that I'm probably going to go back into the chair more—but then I might go into another remission again. Collagen diseases do that, you slip in and out.

How does that feel, when you know you'll be disabled again?
I've never stopped being disabled. But to be *that* handicapped again? It scares me more than anything I've yet dealt

with. Sometimes, it's almost hard to say it, but sometimes I almost wish I had one, stable, traumatic injury. Because I'd know what I could count on. This way, I never know who I'm going to be, where I'm going to be in relation to the disease. I don't know how it will affect my life. Because I live in both worlds I have some special problems. A good example is a couple months ago when I was doing job interviewing. I went for one interview at a school where I was doing an internship as a counselor for the deaf and they said, "Well, you're not going to go into the chair are you? I mean, you're better, right?" So for them, I was too disabled. But two days later, I went to another office for an interview for working with disabled people and their comment was, "Gee, it's a shame you aren't more visibly disabled." For them I wasn't disabled enough. Talk about your double discrimination!

It's a very scary feeling, when I feel myself going back into the wheelchair because I keep getting a taste of what it's like not to have to worry. This apartment is an obvious outshoot from my denying what was going on while I was in remission. I took a second floor apartment and now whenever I'm in the chair, which has been more and more often in the last four months, I can't get into my own home! So, I'm looking for an accessible apartment now. I can't just react out of where I am today, I have to remember tomorrow and yesterday. I could be completely different physically than I am today.

Tell me a bit more about what the organic disease has been like. You said it was a collagen disease?

I must be as nebulous with you as the doctors are with me. It's a collagen-vascular disorder. When it first hit it looked like classic rheumatoid arthritis. It had all the symptoms—the pain, the fever, the sudden weight loss, and the exhaustion. And then, about a year later, I developed problems with breathing and a rash on my face, and they went, ah! *lupus.* And then I developed kidney problems and I was told I was in the terminal stages of lupus. So I went through the whole thing of accepting that I was dying at that point. From there, lab tests were inconclusive. I developed nodules for which they did biopsies, and everything was inconclusive, so they didn't know what that was. So at this point I've got muscle and bone involvement. I've got a really bad bleeding disorder of some kind, but they don't know how that ties in. My liver functions are down. I had very bad kidney stones and my lungs are involved too. A lot of systems are being affected but they don't know why. A couple of months ago I had my first joint "explode" in about two years. It started to deform a little bit. So, the disease is starting to go back into that syndrome, but they don't know what it is. They have no name for it, they just know it's an auto-immune syndrome, and they know it's a collagen-vascular disorder, and they don't know anything else.

I'm not unique, you know. Millions of young women especially and some young men live through this purgatory of a nebulous cluster of symptoms with no identifiable foe. Psychologically it was devastating—I doubted my own ability to reason or believe my own body. Thank God, I tapped into organizations for persons with collagen disorders—it helped me regain that belief in myself no matter how vague the disease—I know what I know; I feel what I feel, diagnosis or no. One of the most complex areas that I deal with now, other than the physical trauma, is the fact that the whole thing has left me with this feeling of having trouble believing in tomorrow. It's made me a little bit more skeptical about how much time I've got to do something. I have always been a fairly intense person, but I know it has kicked my intensity up. I know I have more desire for getting something done and enjoying it and feeling everything that I can right now. Ironically, it also has greatly increased my patience, my tolerance. Sound like a contradiction? My life is chock full of them. It's swinging back and forth and it'll go maybe uphill, maybe downhill. I can go out discoing tonight, you know, and be in wheelchair for the next week as a reaction. I never know exactly what my own limits are going to be, which makes it very easy for me to push myself past my limits. It's been hard, but it's at the point now where that terrible anger isn't there anymore. It's more the frustration of, damnit, why did it have to be *this* morning! But I'm five years into it; I'm more accepting. I'm more accepting, but I still reject it, because of the frustration. Another contradiction! But contradictions are just experiencing both sides of a single thing.

Being disabled is not as traumatic to me now as it was when I first became disabled, because then I had twenty-two years worth of all the biases and prejudices and fears that every able-bodied person has to get past. When I first went into the wheelchair I didn't know what to expect of myself, but once I went into the wheelchair I realized I was still me; I mean, going into the chair didn't change my essence. It made me realize these are human beings with disabilities, not disabled people. This insight was afforded me only because I knew of my own human being suddenly thrown into this "outside" group of beings. As I went into the disabled population more and began to have more intimate feelings with friends, both male and female, the human factor took over. I wasn't as scared of being disabled, because I had found its limits. Prejudice is based on fear. Fear is based on ignorance. Able-bodied and disabled people all have individual personalities, have the same joys or the same communication problems whether able-bodied or disabled. I have as many fights with my disabled gentlemen friends as I do with the able-bodied. And that took the fear of being disabled away because then I knew I could be human and disabled both! God, that sounds so stupid. So corny. But it is at that low a level of emotion. Disability manages to make people blot out their normal impressions of you as a person with intellect, warmth, wit, sexual identity—it all gets covered under this cloak called "crippled."

I think one of the hardest parts was my friends who didn't see the human factor, friends who didn't let me stay myself when I became disabled, especially a man that I loved. He was with me before I became disabled. He met me when I was just going into it. And as I became more seriously involved and much more restricted he was able to be honest enough with me to tell me that he just couldn't deal with that, which at the time I couldn't give him credit for, but I can now. He, in his own pain and anger, had to strike out. He said, "I can't love a cripple, even if it's you," which at the time just devastated me. We tried, for like another year and a half, to work on it, and it got to the point where we were just hurting each other so badly, you know. Again, I must admit I was not unique. Do you know the statistics on loved ones leaving traumatically disabled people? And the rate for disabled women is about six to one being left to cope alone. It is a terribly frightening feeling. It is hard to continue to love yourself when you find you are unlovable to your chosen person. *That* could be a book in itself!

What were some of the problems?

The main problem was that our whole lifestyle had to change. I was just in so much pain that it was affecting a couple of major areas, the first being our social area. I just could not go out and do the activities that we used to be able to do together. I didn't have the stamina. I needed to be home earlier. It affected our sexual aspect. I was in so much pain sometimes I just couldn't make love with him and we went through this whole thing of, "Well, what's going to happen when you're really severely disabled? Are you not going to be able to have sex?" And I'd say, "I don't know." And he would say, "Well if you can't, I'd have to go out and find it where I can." We lost sight of the difference between sex and making love. If we could have stopped the panic we could have seen what we lost was communication—that's when we stopped making love. Sex was just one of the many casualities. And there was the fact that if it was rheumatoid, which we thought at the time, I would become "deformed." He went for prettiness and such. When he couldn't deal with his pain, he used to tell me how bad I looked to him, that I was ugly and deformed in his eyes when he saw me. I mean really painful things to hear but today I believe that was his way of kind of hoping that I would leave the relationship first. We were too weak to be the first to leave one another so we stayed and just tried to make the other one play the villain. I feel so badly about that. If only we could have just said "Listen, I love you, but I cannot deal with the changes. I must leave."

One of the problems that a lot of disabled people have is getting close to somebody in the first place. But you were close to somebody and then became disabled. What kind of a difference did that make?

The difference was that I didn't have the choice. Neither of us had a choice. I didn't meet him and then say, "I have a disability." Then if he had problems dealing with it I could back away before we got to the hurting part. I was committed. I was involved. And so was he. We had no choice. It was forced upon us. That is a fear I face today. Hindsight is so marvelous. I say what I should have done. But, tomorrow, if I fall in love, would I be strong enough to walk away early on if I foresee the pain? I'll have to let you know on that one.

I have a very close, precious friend who has been my friend for over ten years. He and I lived together when we were both very young. I never changed in *his* eyes. When he used to come and deal with me in the chair, you know, he was still dealing with *me*. Today he is still involved in my life. It just never changed for him. So, there are some people who don't have the fear, the anger. He is a much more flexible, more placid man.

As a matter of fact, just last Thursday the man I mentioned who left me due to the disability came back and saw me again and took me out to dinner, and he told me that he had thought about it all these years and he realized that he had never had a love that was as supportive and as good and secure as ours had been — that he still loved me, and he wanted to try it again. And I was just so amazed at that. If I had played that scene in my mind once, I had done so a million times. Scenes of what he would do or what he would say if he ever came back, and, he did it better than if I had written a script! And I was just floating on that. And I was saying to myself, "My God, he finally got to the point where the love was more than the disability." But then I kind of hurt my finger and he asked what happened, and I showed him and said I had had a joint attack. And I saw that look of horror cross his face. And at that point I knew that he had done a very *intellectual* coming to grips with the fact that he still loved me, but when he was faced with the disability again we had to replay that whole fateful scene of three years ago, because emotionally he had not come to grips with the reality of it. But, that was important. I guess that final tying off had to be done.

Interestingly, during a relationship with a man who did have a disability, I found a lot of similarities as well as differences. There was a lot more patience. I don't think there was any less fear, because he was just as scared as I or as the other man of what the outcome could be and of how disabled I could become. But there was an acceptance because that human factor was known to him, being disabled himself. It doesn't seem to really matter if I see disabled or nondisabled men — they all fear the uncertainty of my disease. But there is a huge difference in the acceptance factor. An empathy with my saying "I can't go out tonight, I'm in pain."

It's a terrible pressure no matter who I'm with, because it's just not easy to watch a person that you love be in pain. It's not easy to watch a person that you love go through these things and not be able to do a damn thing. I feel a lot of pain for somebody who cares for me and spends time with me, because I know myself the pain and anguish of having that helpless feeling watching a deterioration. So what I have to do is be very careful to make sure that I let them do what they can for me. I have to be able to accept. I tend to want to, when I'm in my worst attacks, just be alone, just do what I can with it. And that's the worst thing I can do — to alienate the person who loves me at a moment like that. I have to force myself to let them do even something like get the water, get me the aspirin. I have to learn to let someone help me because I first had to learn how to deal with it all alone.

Why do you suppose so many disabled people fall into not being able to accept help?

Well, first of all, you don't know where the help is coming from. If it's coming from guilt or from pity you can just take it and shove it, you know, that's the last kind of help I want. But if they're doing it out of love, and I reject it, that's a terrible thing. So I have to tell where the help is coming from. The second thing is the whole feeling of self-worth, autonomy, and independence. Those three tie in so intricately. You know, how disabled, how handicapped am I going to let this disability make me — for example, I can make it up those stairs on my own, damnit; I'm still that much of a person; I can handle that, you know; I don't need your help, I can make it. So it's that feeling of how much help can I take and still feel that I am an independent person.

I have been pushed by a lot of doctors who say, you can't let this stop you. For instance, even though I no longer am in the chair full time, there are times when the pain or my fever is so bad that I don't have the stamina I need to keep going through my meetings and my work. So I use the chair to conserve energy. When I've got fifteen minutes worth of energy if I walk, maybe I can make it through two more hours if I'm in the chair just by being able to put the energy into a different direction. I don't have to put the energy into holding down the pain *and* walking, I can put the energy into my interactions with people. One doctor will understand that. Endorse it. But the next doctor will say, But you don't need the chair right now because you can still walk. So I get all these mixed messages of, take care of yourself, be careful, do what you need to do to preserve yourself; and the next one is saying, you wanna play cripple? But that's that whole thing that I've been through, with having a foot in both worlds. People try to impose their moral judgments on you. Do I fit their criteria of strong or weak? Respected or pitied?

Independence does not mean you have to do everything that you're capable of doing alone and accept whatever it is that you cannot do alone. As long as I'm putting out a hundred percent effort I'm still a fully independent person even if it may be only eighty percent or ten percent in your eyes. I don't have to do it alone to be independent. Independent also means being able to accept the fact that I've got limitations, accept that as part of myself. If I have to call somebody up on the phone and say I need help with this, I haven't lost my independence. Rather, I've simply gained my dependence.

Independence is a really funny issue in the disabled movement right now. For example, this one man I know who was deaf told me how in the schools for the deaf, one of the ways that they trained deaf children to be independent is to put them in these dormitories with very stark walls. They aren't allowed to have pretty, funny things on the walls because they're visual and that would distract them and encourage them to daydream. So they would force them into this sterile environment to build better "independence." But what I see is that they were setting up these people to be very lonely, and shutting off one of their greatest enjoyments in life, which is visual effect. Independence has got to be redefined, because the way we have it defined right now we're setting people up for failure. Independence should not equate solitude.

Let's go back to something. Despite what you said about the human factor, do you have a different way of thinking and acting being disabled than you did when you were able-bodied?

The humanity is the foundation, and the disabled or able-bodied personality is the house that is built on top of that foundation. When the disability hit, it was like a tornado came in and ripped down my house. The house that I could rebuild was totally different from the one that I had built before. But with that same foundation. Remember what I said about a sister self? I went through a terrible shift in terms of self-image. And when your self-image is zip, there's no way you can interact with other people on a strong basis. So what I've had to do is rebuild my self-image, and in rebuilding my self-image I had to build in that I could be very beautiful, even if my body is "deformed," even if I am in a wheelchair. Even though this joint in my finger is deformed, when I touch somebody that I love they're able to feel my love. My finger may look different, but my hands can still do what they were always able to do in terms of sharing with somebody or doing a job, whether it be work or love or whatever. They're still able to do what I need them to be. They just look different.

There are parts of myself that I really love. I'm really a terrific empathetic. Do you remember an episode on *Star Trek* where Kirk, Spock, and McCoy were put onto this planet where there were these beings who would inflict pain, and then this young woman empathetic could come over and put her hands on them and draw their pain out and absorb it? I liken myself to that. In my counseling, at points I can really feel what that person is feeling and I'm able to tell them that. I'm able to share that with them in such a fashion that they are able to get into that pain or that pleasure more. And that has made me a really good counselor. It's also made me a really good friend, because when my friends need to really feel joy or really feel sadness, I really laugh with them and I really cry with them and it's all honest. It's hard because it takes me to a lot of extremes; it's very exhausting, but I would never give it up. I love it in myself—the ability to really feel what other people feel.

And I love my ability to laugh. I can usually find the really humorous side of something. I can let my child out. I can let my adult out and I can let my parent out, but I can let my child out and that's a gift. It's beautiful because I can really play hard and I need to play hard. And I've got just a beautiful relationship in terms of my own belief of "God." I figure She or He has the best sense of humor of us all, and I'm able to talk to God as I would to a friend. And that's great, because I feel like I've got some sort of communication where I can vent the good and the bad. I can praise God in everything She/He does, but I can praise God and hate God both. Just like I can tell somebody, I love you, but I don't like you right now. Or even tell someone I hate them as I love them. It's all a part of that being able to experience both sides of a single issue.

I guess the thing I like the most about myself is the fact that I can love *so* much. I've got a real deep well of love that I can tap into. Sometimes I am amazed how deeply I can feel things.

I don't like parts of myself that have not been able to grow and change. I don't like the parts of myself that are afraid of a lot of things. That holds me back in a lot of areas. I have to fight these really bad fears. I mean everything, from fear of elevators (which for a person in a wheelchair is just devastating), to fear of something off the wall such as finding drugs in the punch at a party. Old tapes instilled into me. Irrational fears. Becoming disabled the way I did—no warning, no reason, no clear cut anything, escalated my ability to have irrational fear. For good reasons, because it was a blow out of the blue—but the difference here is that the old tapes were taught—the new fear was thrust upon me and I could fight back with my accumulated strength and experience in life. Stop the tape before it becomes a permanent part of my collection!

Most of the things you like or dislike about yourself were there before the disability. Are there any parts of yourself that you like or that you dislike as a result of the disability?

The part I don't like about myself as a result of the disability is the weakness area of being a disabled person—not being able to do what I want to do when I want to do it, because of the barriers set up by society. Also, being in so much pain that it just gets to the point where it spills out on somebody who's near me, whether I have to take some time and bitch about it, or whether I'm not telling them I'm in pain and then they do something and I snap at them. The fact that my life is not the only life that is affected by my disability, that whoever's near me is going to be affected by my disability frustrates me. I don't like being disabled in terms of the restrictions that it puts on my life. I was disabled later in life, I'm only five years into my new pattern. I have a lot of friends who are a million times more severely disabled than I am and they live with it far better because they were born disabled. They have built up more of an acceptance. They have other angers that I don't have, because of the discrimination they faced their whole life through. I mean, it's a trade-off, so I don't consider myself any better off than them, or them any better off than me. It's just a trade-off. They just have different areas of pain and anger than I do.

The part of myself that I like better now is that in the midst of this terrible crisis when I thought that my whole life was coming to a standstill, everything I ever wanted or needed in life seemed to be ending. It goes something like this. "In the midst of darkest winter I found inside of myself an indomitable summer." I became disabled and I went through the loss of my man and I went through that whole fear of dying and I continued in college and I got my two degrees and I came up here and I worked on getting my next degree and I continued to work and I found out that I am a *gutsy,* strong lady. And I never knew I was! I thought I was a weak, little woman who was scared of everything in life. And I'm not! And I don't know if I would have found that out if I hadn't become disabled. That whole theory of we only use a tenth of our brain? I think we only use a tenth of our strength, and our beliefs, and our feelings. We are taught very early on by society to deal on this real surface level with ourselves and with others. And once you break through that surface tension, you know that little skim on the top of the pudding, and you dive down in, there's this huge, huge vat of strength. And I think at least eighty-five percent of the people would have it. People say, "I could never do what you've done, Doe." But that is just their fear speaking.

Did you find that through your faith in God?

Before, religion was something I was afraid to admit to ascribing to. I denied how much God meant to me because I really rejected the establishment and conformity of formalized religion. I lost a lot of my contact and my joy and my strength in what I had with God. But when I became disabled and I went through that whole period of deep introspection, and had to come to grips with what is left of me that I like that I wanted to polish and build on—I found religion was one of my strengths, one of my joys.

Does that make religion a crutch?

It might, sure. I imagine that religion is a crutch. Any belief is a crutch. Belief in tomorrow is a crutch if you want to carry it out to that extreme. But to me, getting back into the independent thing, a crutch does not mean lack of independence, it just means, hey, it's crutch time, okay, I need a crutch. We all need crutches once in a while, because we are not totally invincible. We are not one hundred percent pure dynamo strength. We have a lot of weaknesses and a lot of vices where help is really wonderful to get. I could probably do it alone perfectly well, but I can do it in half the time and with half the pain and half the anguish if I take some help. And that includes God.

Back to your body. How do you feel different about yourself when you're in the chair and when you're standing up?

That really requires two answers. The first is how I feel about me in relation to myself. I feel a loss of control and stifled. I have to shift my emphasis from physical to more cerebral. Use different outlets for my energy. The second is myself in relation to others. People react to me differently, vastly differently, when I'm in the chair. They seem to feel I am not able to do all I'm capable of doing when I'm not standing erect. If something is wrong with my body, then something must be wrong with my mind and being. And because that changes day to day, I'm never able to fully accept my new limitations. When I'm standing up I've got all these limitations taken away; I can go this far again, and then all of a sudden I'm back in the chair. I've had to develop a flexibility with myself as well as with others.

It's really screwed up my whole idea of time, because time before was measured by days, hours, minutes. But now time is my greatest friend and my worst enemy. Time is how long I'm going to be able to go today before I'm back in the chair. Time is how many days I'm going to be in the chair before I'm out again. Time is how many days I'm going to be able to live. Time is a lot more of a boundary than it was before.

I don't mind being disabled, but I don't like being handicapped. I don't like the fact that my environment becomes a barrier as opposed to just being my environment. The disability itself is not my problem. My problem is the limitations in my environment that make it a handicap. One of the main things that I can offer to the people that I work with is that I am a very feeling and sensitive person and when someone is going through some really bad pain and they need to be held or touched I can respond. But if I'm in the wheelchair it's harder to hold them or touch them, especially if they're in a chair too. It's hard to get that closeness when you're both in chairs just because of logistics. Or if they fear my chair and therefore fear my touch because of it, that is a barrier. Or if there's a medical emergency that I need to do something about and I'm in the chair I feel a lot more restricted in being able to carry through what I know I can do. In personal life, if I've accepted a dinner invitation with a friend, and then the night of the dinner I'm in the chair — if they know me fine, but if it's a new person, and there I am sitting in the wheelchair, then I have to go through that whole thing of — "Well, why don't you come in and we'll have a drink and we'll talk a little bit; I know this is a surprise and it's just a part of me you don't know yet." If he or she decides they want to go ahead and go out, is the place accessible?

I guess one common reaction of most other people, at least I've noticed it in relation to me, is a reaction to your pain.

Oh, God, yes. They're afraid to touch you if you're in the wheelchair. You're sick, you see, if you're disabled. But especially me, because I'm in pain.

Well, what's it like to be in that kind of pain?

Well, I got more in touch with it just this past week, as a matter of fact, because I've been going through a stage where I'm doing an awful lot of bleeding, I'm doing a lot of bruising. So, the doctor told me to stop all aspirin, and I've had to go without aspirin and other pain killers, which limits my functioning a lot. So I have been off aspirin for over a week (I was taking between twelve and eighteen aspirin a day) and I have had to come to grips in a whole new way with my pain. I was sitting at work the other day, and I was just almost vibrating with the pain. I just wanted to scream! One of the women I work with came over to me and said she could really see I was in terrible pain. I stopped and just got in touch with it, and I started crying. I told her I felt like a little animal in the forest that stepped into one of those steel traps. It's got me. And I can't think clearly, I can't react fast. This steel trap is on me, but I can't gnaw off my paw and get out of the trap. And that's how it feels to be in that kind of pain, I've got a part of me in this steel trap.

I'm in a lot of pain right now. What I'm usually able to do is go through this morning ritual. When I wake up in the morning—that's when the pain is worse, you know, because I've been a long time without the aspirin—I'll lie there and acknowledge my pain first. I'll get in touch with all the parts of myself that hurt, and I'll let myself feel the pain and the anguish and hurt, and then I'll start to go through some movement and get myself going and go and take a hot shower and take my aspirin. In my mind I use a lot of mental imagery. I close my eyes, and the really bad pain spots glow red, and I walk through my body and take all the red spots and gather them, and then put them in this little box back here and close the box. And then I go. I know where the pain is, but I've got it controlled. But without the aspirin, without the locks, these little red spots have jumped out and one will sneak out and all of a sudden I'll be sitting there, and you know, I'll realize that one of those little red spots is there, and I'll have to sit and mentally nurture it: it's pain, it hurts, that's terrible, come on, come on, come on, get in the box, get in the box, get in the box!

I'm not able to react to you with as much energy as I could normally because I have to take a lot of energy just holding down the pain. I've got a lot of things that are happening today, the coalition meeting, there's errands I have to run, and I'm going to be dead by about six, seven o'clock tonight. I mean the pain is going to take over pretty much.

But part of my adaptation process, and it's very important to me, is that I don't relate to you through my disability first. So I've got a smile on my face because it's a beautiful day! I had a really fun afternoon when I had a cream pie fight yesterday with a friend! I had a really nice evening last night. I'm in pain, but I'm very happy. You can do both you know! The pain is a factor to me, but I don't let it be the foremost factor.

Before I was disabled if I got sick, or I got an infection, or I had a terrible headache or a toothache, because it was something different, I gave myself over to pain because when we're sick we suffer. But when it's chronic pain, to hand myself over at twenty-seven years of age to the pain, that scares me to death! I would lose myself!

Back to other people's reaction to you flipping in and out.
Okay, when I deal with people when I'm out of the chair,

they more easily react to the person that I am. What they see is a young woman coming in for whatever business, be it professional or as a friend, and they will just take the time to learn who I am and what I'm putting across. When I come in with the chair, they react first out of their own fear and prejudices toward the factor of the disability, and I have to fight to get them to a point where they will learn who I am as a person. First, I have to let them work through their own fears and prejudices. Some of them can't get away from the fact that I'm in the chair. This varies whether I meet a disabled person or an able-bodied person too. If I meet a disabled person and I'm not in the chair and we're talking and I say, "Yeah, we disabled people...," they sort of look at me and think, she doesn't look very disabled—she must have epilepsy or she must have a learning disability or diabetes, or something. And then as we're talking later and I say, "Yeah, you know, when I'm in the chair...," they say, "When you're in the *chair*?" I get this ambivalent feeling from disabled people in terms of—well, God, you're a lucky stiff; you can get out of the chair. And sometimes I'll meet their anger or their bitterness at the fact that I can be out of the chair. And that hurts me, because they don't understand the seriousness of my own disability.

Like I was saying, I would rather have one stable disability. I'd know what I could count on. There's a luck factor in that I can walk, I mean I don't want to discount the fact that I sometimes have full mobility. But I would trade that off tomorrow if I could count on what my own limitations were, and know where I was going to be from day to day or from hour to hour. That feeling of living in flux is the real handicap.

What happens when people meet you when you're not disabled and later on when you are disabled, and vice versa?

Well, as I said before, it depends on how we met the first time, as professional or personal friends. If you met me first when I'm not in the chair and I impressed you with the research we were talking about and we decided we were going to get back together and help each other on a project, and I come in that day for the meeting in the chair, you get a little bit scared at first, then say, "What happened, did you fall down the stairs?" And then once I tell you about the disease, a lot of times, to be honest, one of the reaction is—"Wow, I have a lot of respect for you."

If you met me as a person, as a female, and develop some sort of relationship first, that's a whole different kettle of fish, because now you have to deal with the question of — do I want to take out a disabled woman? I mean, you think, my God! what else is wrong with her, what else does this affect? How else has she changed since I met her? She's a whole different person now. So what I have to do then is talk to you and reassure you I am still me. Then I must figure out why you want to take me out. I have to figure out if you still want to go out with *me,* whether you really like me and you really want to spend some time with me anyway, or whether you're doing it out of pity, or whether you're doing it out of just interest. Dating someone disabled can be an adventure. Like dating someone black. But that isn't always negative. It can be a true growth and awareness experience. I can handle that sometimes!

Let's say you've met me a couple of times before and you come in and see me in the chair for the first time. Usually the person says, "What happened?" And I say "Well, something happened, but it happened five years ago. Would you like a cup of coffee and we'll talk about it?" And I'll give the story of how five years ago the disease set in, and this is the way it's affecting me and this is the problem that I have with it today. So then after I'm done saying that, and you've asked me a few questions, I'll say something to the effect that I want you to know that you really do have the option of being able to take some time and think about how you feel about this. If you would like to spend some more time tonight, we can just sort of get to know each other a little bit more; if you want to go out and continue with the plans that's fine, but I also can cook us some dinner in, and we can just have some time alone and get to know each other. But if you're feeling a little bit overwhelmed right now, then what I'd invite you to do is just think about it and then you can get back in touch with me. I really would like to offer you the time and the space to do what you need to do because I've had five years to deal with this and you're only ten minutes into it.

I've had some people say, "Well, I'd still like to spend some time with you, but you know, I was gonna take you to a movie." If the movie house isn't accessible, I'll just help them come up with options: maybe there's something on TV, or maybe we could play Scrabble. I've also had a person say they really need to think about this. And that's really okay, but I want them to leave knowing that I'm really glad that they offered me the time to get to know them better, and if they'll still like to meet later, I would too. I make sure that I touch them one more time before they leave, so that they get the human factor.

I do identify myself as a disabled person. It's not something that I have to try to disguise. Whether I'm on my feet or not I'm *not* an able-bodied person; I'm a disabled person who can walk sometimes. And that is carried over in my work, in my counseling skills, in helping people come to grips with their own disabilities or in my personal life. My life is at the point where everything important I do revolves around the disabled emphasis.

Do you think that's a loss compared to what you would be doing otherwise?

Not really. I was going into medical school because I wanted to be able to help people. I wanted to help to ease illness and sickness and do preventive medicine and cures, and I'm doing that. I mean I'm not working on your body, but I'm in the same field, I'm just in a different aspect of it. My work is preventive medicine for society's ills—just not physical ones! So it hasn't been a big change. If anything, I think it's good because I think I'm really good in administration. I'm really good in negotiation. I'm really good in the interpersonal skills. As a doctor, I would have been good in the research area, but I think I might be even better in administration than I would have been in research. I have a new job now. I'm the director of the Office of Handicapped Affairs for the City of Boston Department of Health and Hospitals. Working as a 504 compliance officer, I use all my skills as well as my personal insight as a disabled person.

Have you ever felt discrimination in jobs and school?

Oh yes, I felt discrimination in jobs in the sense that when I became initially disabled, again this is pre-504, I was not given the chance to try and work out modifications. And that story of my own double discrimination recently. I should clarify 504: I am talking about Section 504 of the Rehabilitation Act of 1973. That is the civil rights act, so to speak, for persons with disabilities. It is a federal law that prohibits discrimination on the basis of disability. It states that no person shall, based upon her or his handicap, be denied entrance into, participation in, or the benefits of any program receiving federal funds. In my office, I work with both employment issues for the worker as well as the actual health care delivery system to patients. I work to insure equal access to the system. It is an awesome job — but then it is a very powerful piece of federal legislation. We have a long history of discrimination to overcome. All the barriers we face — architectural, educational, employment — all are based on the attitudinal barriers. That fear and prejudice we spoke of comes from ignorance. For so long people with disabilities were this group out there we just sort of pitied and gave our dimes to help. Today we work to help people understand we are over twenty percent of the population. Also, we are the only minority with open admission! I joined at twenty-two. Others at birth. Still others later when they become elderly. But we are all people at all levels of society who are not striving to be given privileges, but simply to be allowed our rights as citizens with a lot to live and do in life. As I look back on it now, I think I could have maintained my old job as a biology lab teaching assistant and just utilized my student aides in a different way, but still have done what I did in terms of the tutoring and the working. But I lost the job when I became disabled. I also feel now I could have, if I had wanted to, stayed in medical school. One of the women who was a student at the college — where I worked in the Disabled Student Center — has now graduated and just got accepted at Harvard Medical School. She is paraplegic. The discrimination that I faced when I became disabled can be alleviated for other people through the use of legislation, through the changes via 504, which says, you've gotta give us a chance to equal access to the world we live in. 504 isn't the answer. Legislation never is an answer in and of itself. But it's a tool. It's a tool that gets us a foot in the door to at least explain how accommodations could be made. The only thing 504 gives me is leverage. It will now get me or my clients into an employer's office, but then it's a responsibility once in the door to determine whether or not something's going to happen.

Anything else to say?

I think I've covered a lot of the aspects about myself that I wanted you to know. It is not easy for me to say a lot of these things knowing that people will read it. I am a private person. To speak of my pain, my frustration and weaknesses, even my sexuality, is very hard for me. But I think that this book is a symbol of all I've tried to work for. Now I have made a very personal commitment to my work. Knowledge is the way to prevent prejudice, to modify prejudice. If people are able to read a book of interviews with "disabled people" and realize they are people first — disabilities are a tiny aspect — then I will have widened the human factor a touch more in life.

Don Galloway

"We hold these truths to be self-evident, that all men are created equal, that they are endowed by their Creator with certain unalienable Rights, that among these rights are Life, Liberty, and the pursuit of Happiness."

Since these ringing phrases, crafted just over two centuries ago to open the Declaration of Independence and the newly United States' existence, society has in some ways changed so that the parties to the social contract include not only men, but women. Not only whites, but blacks. Not only people with able bodies, but disabled people.

But in other ways, the country has not changed, in part still living by these same self-evident truths and for the other part constantly asserting and reasserting their promise. The social and political enfranchisement of blacks, women, disabled people, and other minorities has not come easily. Intense effort by those minorities and by the society of which they are part was required. While enfranchisment is not complete, while racism, sexism, and other bigotries exist, Americans have in some significant measure succeeded in recognizing that their nation includes all those people in it.

Some may find it a new idea to conceive of the disabled as a minority group, perhaps once thinking of them as "sick." But they suffer the same prejudices, underemployment, poor education, and stigmatization that are suffered by other minority groups. Some may be tired of the public attention received by minority groups. Yet another minority group may seem too much. Yet as the people tire, the disabled are denied a self-evident humanity.

181

Whether the disabled minority is able to achieve inclusion in the American social contract is a question to which the answer is now being decided. Now the legal mandate is clear. Public Law 94-142, the Education for all Handicapped Children act, provides disabled children with the right to a public education long presumed by most but heretofore denied to most children if they were disabled. Section 504 of the Rehabilitation Act of 1973 mandating equal opportunity for handicapped people has been referred to as the "civil rights law" for the disabled. These two milestones in federal legislation have signaled a new era for disabled people, recognizing them and including them as parties to the social contract.

But the social contract is not only written in the words of the law. It is also written in the actions of society. Without changes here, legislation can be empty. Still, the legislation itself has caused issues concerning disability to become more visible as well as disabled people themselves.

As with other minority groups, the inclusion of the handicapped into the social contract has required and will continue to require intense effort on the part of disabled people, their parents, concerned professionals and society at large.

Society is crucial. For although there is an obvious biological reality to disability, the significance of this biology to all concerned, disabled and able-bodied, pales beside the social interpretation of that biology. Here too there is a parallel with race and sex. Although these both have a biological reality, the significance of biology is overwhelmed by those social interpretations we call racism or sexism. It is the overwhelmingly social nature of disability that makes it possible—and indeed necessary—to renegotiate the social contract. That social contract of tomorrow shall regard all as equal and all as having the unalienable rights earlier declared. It shall be a social contract, written and unwritten, that includes those who, like the some 40 million disabled citizens of this country, are different.

Don Galloway is a 36-year-old active blind black man who has devoted most of his mature life to understanding and defeating the purely social aspects of disability.

I went to regular schools until I was twelve, and then during that summer I got shot with a bow and arrow and infection set in. Bad medical treatment and a bad social welfare system prevented me from getting proper care. I was put into a state school for the blind, and by the time I was sixteen I had lost my sight completely.

What happened is that I was playing in the backyard with a bunch of kids. We would get together, about fifteen of us, boys, and we would play cowboys and Indians and hunt each other all over the neighborhood — we had woods, and little creeks, and little bushes — and I got shot in the eye with a bow and arrow. It was on a Sunday and my parents took me to someone and he looked at my eye and said that everything was going to be all right and he patched it up and cleaned it out. I went back because I started to have tremendous headaches and my sight was getting worse. My eye was running and it looked infected, so I went back and he cleaned it out, but instead of giving me penicillin he gave me a prescription for glasses. This was all billed to welfare, so there may not have been a real interest on his part, cause it wasn't economically profitable for him.

My parents got me into Johns Hopkins cause that's a medical facility for welfare and a teaching college, so they would let strange cases come there. I would spend all day long going back and forth from this awful Johns Hopkins to the general eye clinics. One thing they found was that the prescription for the glasses was wrong. My eyes were acting up really bad, hurting me, and I was taking drops and stuff like that.

Then I went to stay on my uncle's tobacco farm, and they took me over to Duke University, where they said what they needed to do was to take one eye out to save the other eye. For some strange reason if you get shot and one eye gets infected the other eye will respond to it and get infected, so you not only lose sight in one eye, you lose sight in both. At that time the treatment was to take out one eye. Right now the treatment is to puncture one eye and do a trip with the other eye to save it. The thing is that they have enough drugs now to knock it right out. They could have knocked it out if I had had penicillin from the start, and they could have knocked it out at the secondary stage if they had taken the eye out, but because I wasn't a citizen of the state I had to go back to my home to get medical treatment. By the time I got back there, it took about a week to get back cause my family was poor and we had to arrange transportation and all that stuff, the damage was really bad and I got put immediately into Johns Hopkins hospital.

Are you a little bit angry about all that?

Well, I'm angry in a general sense, but I don't personalize it in a traumatic sense cause I don't think blindness is a terrible thing. As a matter of fact, since I lost my sight I have had a lot of fun. I've been able to do a lot of things, I've been able to travel, I've been able to meet beautiful people, I've just had a ball to be very honest with you. I lost my sight at a young age, at thirteen, but it wasn't a traumatic thing to me cause my neighborhood accepted me, all the girls accepted me and all the guys. My family was large, five brothers and two sisters, and they said, well, you're blind, big deal, you'll have to go out and make it. So blindness wasn't a traumatic difference in my lifestyle.

It broadened my lifestyle because all of a sudden I went to the blind schools, I could be free from my family. I didn't have to have my parents say yes or no every time I wanted to go into the city, I could just go. I had a little money in my pocket that I would hustle up by washing dishes in the school, so I would go and do my trip on weekends. I learned my own mobility and my own social skills.

When we moved to California in fifty-four I was used to being independent. I went to the Foundation for the Junior Blind when it first started, and I had a chance to go yachting, take airplane trips, go on trips down to Mexico and be exposed to all kinds of entertainment.

My family was not that involved in digging out resources for me because they were busy trying to survive, to feed us, to get us rent for the house. But I always took the initiative to do it myself, and I found out that I could get into junior high school, and then I graduated from there and graduated from city college and lived in Los Angeles. I went on the road entertaining (I was a professional entertainer for three years with National School Assemblies), got my master's, and then went out of the country for two years and did research in South and Central America.

Education was free, I just had it made, so it wasn't a big upset with me, and I don't have the personal bitterness that you would suspect I would have. But I'm very uptight about how the American medical system runs, you know, the inequities of the system. I'm not upset about it because of my blindness, but because of my humanness. I think that good medical treatment should be available to everybody that's living. It's a system thing, not a white or black thing. What happened to me, I think, would have happened to a poor white kid, or anybody in the same economic situation that I was in. The system was not set up to handle people that couldn't pay for it. I don't think that the treatment that Johns Hopkins gave me was based on my blackness, it was based on my economics.

What is your professional background?

I have a master's in social work in the area of community planning and experience in organizing a complete health delivery system—I worked with the department of community medicines as an assistant director of community health projects. I have worked extensively with all of the blind groups, national and local, in Los Angeles, San Diego, and in Central and South America. I got involved with the National Federation for the Blind, so I know their philosophy and their power structure and some of their goals and objectives, and also with the ABC group, the Associated Blind of California. I spoke at their last conference on how to involve the blind consumer in his own processes, and I used to work with the Foundation for the Junior Blind.

What kind of work do you do now?

Right now I'm coordinator for services for the blind. I do planning for the basic services we offer, like reading services, transportation, mobility, advocacy, sometimes housing and things like that. But I found that those are just standard services and there is nothing too innovative about getting a reader. The basic philosophy here is, of course, not just to do for folks, but to have folks do for themselves. So what I did was some planning around getting monies to identify where the blind people are in this city, and to get them involved in the whole process of problem solving for themselves, like how to find a job, how to get involved at a political level, how to take care of yourself.

Can you tell me some of the questions they ask you and the kinds of things you tell them?

Sometimes they want to know how they can get involved. For instance, how can they get around to a cultural event, you know, what's around that's intellectual that they can go to with other blind people or alone, or how can they really feel like they have some self worth, really get their own interests going. Or there may be a question about where to find a job or meet a woman. What I automatically do is try to explore their own resources. First, what have they done, what are their contacts, what kinds of things do they want to get involved in, how much mobility do they have, do they have friends — just find out where they are coming from first. And then I try to match up what I know to what they know. It may mean, if they don't know how to get from A to Z that our mobility instructor will come out on a day to work with them. We have a personal staff that can help with any SSI problems, welfare problems, financial problems, anything that has to do with advocacy. We have another personal staff that will help with matching up reading services or attendant services, and another person that may help with housing or transportation. If they want to have an apartment, I take their name and phone number and all the data that I need, and then I just go to talk to them and try to get them involved in calling people, just try to show them ways that they can approach themselves.

Your job deals with the blind, but the organization you work for has brought different types of handicapped people together to work as a coalition. How do you feel about blindness being grouped with other disabilities?

I think I bring a sense of purpose to the whole coalition between the disabled population and the blind. I think that the whole concept of disabled is really that we are disadvantaged people in terms of our blindness, blackness, our disabledness, or whatever. We are all disadvantaged. I feel that if we are going to survive on a social and economic level we have to get together politically, and politically we can be much stronger together as a coalition than separately fighting for our own little things. Now there are aspects of blindness that you don't have to deal with, and aspects of disabledness, like wheelchairs, that I don't have to deal with, but there are certain overriding considerations that are common to both of us.

I'm talking about attitudinal things that society has about

our disabledness, like that being disabled somehow diminishes us as humans. They put us into certain classifications, they treat us a certain way, they discriminate against us because we are in a wheelchair, or we are black, or we are disabled, or we're blind, you know. There's mobility problems that we may have that are common like architectural barriers, and then the job discrimination thing.

Actually the blind have had a lot of political muscle. They are quite organized. And I think the reason the blind are more organized than other groups is that blindness, in my opinion now, is one of the least disabilities. Any relatively intelligent human being can learn mobility. If a person is physically blind, but has all of the other faculties—he can hear good, and feel good, and think well—and if he has the opportunities to advance himself, he can really function quite efficiently. There are some things that get in his way—he can't drive a car, he can't spot all the pretty women all the time—but I really think that blindness has been overplayed in our society as *the* worst thing that can happen to you.

What if you had been born blind?

I don't know. I think sometimes being blind from birth is more damaging than becoming blind afterwards. My family had a chance to know me as a boy without the other added thing of being blind. And when I became blind it was secondary to me. It's hard to say. I think that the people that lose their sight when they're kids may have a better chance cause they have a better perspective of what sight is all about, and your parents have a better conception of what you are because they have seen you not just as a blind person.

Personally, I feel that it is very helpful to be born black and into a big family. My family was very close in the sense that it helped me. My father had a radio program and he used to sing spirituals in a quartet, so we had quartets and choirs right in my family. It was very positive to be black. Also people have been nice to me, my family, number one, has been nice by not separating me out. And my community, being a very close-knit community, they all knew me when I was a kid, they treated me like, you know—he's blind, so big deal, he's doing fine and still getting around. I ran all around my neighborhood, and when you would go between people's houses they would be in their kitchen cooking and you would speak to them and talk. It was just a close thing. All my peer group was positive. Oh, I would get kids that would tease me, but they would tease me because that was their nature, they were teasers anyway. And I would tease them back. So I have had a lot of positive things happen to me.

There are a lot of phrases from the black movement and I was just thinking of what they would mean in the disabled movement, like black is beautiful — is disabled beautiful?

It's the same concept but using different words. Disabled is capable, or disabled has potential. Disabled can be a positive thing. Being black or disabled can bring an added dimension to the realities of life. They are similar in many ways. And disabledness can be a beautiful trip. You can be blind and be beautiful. Hell, yeah, blindness is beautiful. Not in itself, but we have made it that, a positive thing.

Okay, let's try a few others. What about black power — is there disabled power?

Yeah, indeed. That's the only way that we can bring about major changes in our lifestyle, in our potential. A man without power is a very sad man. With power you can do a lot of things. If there is enough power to send a man to the moon, there is enough power to put together a wheelchair that can run by itself or to develop a system to propel a blind man through the streets of a city.

Black pride — is there a disabled pride?

Yeah, the reason that there is a disabled pride is that pride comes with whatever you've done with what you've got. We all have a certain range of capabilities, but we all start from different points. If I can take something that I have that is generally looked upon as a negative and turn that into a very positive thing, I have a pride in that. I have pride in knowing that I can develop myself to any degree. I'm a blind man that did it, and other blind people can do it too. When I go to a convention and see a blind judge, a blind lawyer, or if I see a blind mechanic, I identify with him because he's a human, number one, but also a human being that overcame a lot of things. I feel good cause I identify with them. Even if all I did was come down this hill, I feel proud of that, yeah.

Can black or disabled people be integrated into the main-stream society?

I think that disabled people want the same rights as blacks — human rights. I want to be able to go any place I want to go. I want to be able to go to any school. I want to be able to go to any public place. I want to be able to go to any restaurant. The difference is that the disabled population wants to be integrated into the larger society on all levels, social, economic, political. As a black person, I really don't care if I'm integrated with a white person in that sense, on a social basis, I couldn't care less. I think black people now are not really pushing for social integration. We're looking more for employment and political power. We're looking for the ability to decide what we want as an ethnic group.

I think that disabledness is secondary to me being black. Blackness has a broader appeal to me than me being blind, you know. I think I can be much more comfortable in an all black setting than I could be with an all blind setting.

What does the women's liberation movement mean to you as a disabled man?

I think that the more liberated a person is the better chance I have to be liberated. Women are looking at the images, well let's put it right out front, that white men have set up as perfect, and are saying, hey enough of that nonsense, you're not a God to us, we have our value as women, and there's value in a man having some female characteristics too — there is value in a man crying, a man asking for help, in a man saying, I can't do it. Of course, recognizing the human quality of us all has to include me, and that's me as a blind person, me as a disabled person. Hopefully they can understand that I have been discriminated against just like they have, and they can kind of say, hey, brother, let's talk with each other. I just see it going hand in hand. If one person is oppressed, guess who's going to be next folks. The more a woman is out to find herself the more I can find myself because if I find myself without my woman finding herself then I'm just jiving because half of me is missing.

On a personal basis, because women traditionally have been oppressed — forced into certain roles, certain reactions, certain capabilities — they seem to tune into me. You know, they feel that they can identify with that a little bit. They have that underlying feeling for you because of the stuff that they have to go through. And I recognize that they have a need level also, to be understood, listened to, respected, and loved. I can understand the women's lib thing easily, it is easy for me to tune into that. But the one thing that I always want them to understand is not to get so bitter, so hard. There is a softness there, a warmness there, a beauty there, but if you put up a shell too hard no one is going to try to take time to develop it and cultivate it.

I think that's something that I learned because I've seen blind people get bitter behind their blindness, get turned off by life because of their blindness or disabledness. Black, blind, disabled, we have a tendency as human beings to try to protect ourselves and the best way is to have a hard outside and to become hostile ourselves. But that's self-defeating because if you become very uptight and hostile in an uptight and hostile environment it just escalates, it perpetuates itself and it becomes self-fulfilling prophecies.

What kind of advice would you give a blind child?

Number one, try to learn your environment, learn how people feel and think; study your environment, learn how to react to it. Well first learn yourself, get to feel good about yourself, but learn your environment cause your environment is part of yourself. You cannot separate yourself from your environment.

Number two, be aggressive. You have got to be aggressive, go out after what you think you want to do. You can't wait for other people to do things for you. If you fail, get up and try again, and don't get bitter because you got knocked in the teeth. Go with the expectation that you might get hit and you might be knocked down, and if you can get up, get up and try again. And if you can't then lay down until you recuperate, but keep pushing, keep on shoving. If you stop trucking someone will run you over, or you are going to be pushed to the side. If you are going to function and develop yourself, you have got to make the initial step yourself.

I think that disabled people and blind people should expose themselves to every situation that is not going to be harmful to them. If it means that you are going to hurt yourself and you know it, don't do it. But if you think you might hurt yourself, there's a possibility of hurting yourself, don't let that stop you. Like I traveled all over Central and South America, and some blind people have traveled all over the world with their canes, just tripping around. Other people have said that it wasn't possible, that it's dangerous, there are pits, there are holes. But don't let fear stop you from what you want to do. I think the biggest problem of disabled people, and people as a whole, is that they don't want to expose themselves to life—life is dangerous. But the biggest enemy that you can have is yourself. You have to put away that disadvantagedness and say, okay, I may be misunderstood, I may get hurt, but I am gonna do it, and do it.

A Policy Epilog

Transportation

It is essential to recognize that disabled people exist and to hear their voices before designing public policy. By its narrowest definition, public policy redeems failures in the private market sector by collective governmental action. If the private sector will not undertake building roads and railways and securing safe airports, the government must. When questions of energy efficiency suggest a reworking of national transportation policy, one of the questions that must be raised concerns the use of transportation by disabled people.

Imagine a day in your life. Certain aspects of it can be described by the paths you took—a walk downstairs, a bus trip, etc.—or by the endpoints of the paths—you had breakfast out, went to work. Rational policy will provide means of transportation and will see to it that there are places to which to be transported. The latter requirement has been traditionally provided for in the United States by private policy; public policy complements by completing the former. But with disabled people private policy may not provide the destinations. It may not provide accessible movies, it may have discriminatory barriers against employment. Public policy may furthermore not provide the means for getting to transportation accessible to the disabled even if such exists. The number of wheelchair people who use the wheelchair-accessible Bay Area Rapid Transit (BART) system are considerably fewer than the number who presumably would use it if they had places to go and if they had means of easy access from their apartments to BART.

193

Many, although certainly not all, handicapped people are transportation-disabled. Transportation disability is as complex a concept as any disability. Like work disability, it expresses a relationship between an organized social system and a unique individual. We all rely on our mobility and tend to take it, like our bodies, for granted. Although not expressly stated in the American Constitution, or in any other document (a right so taken for granted presumably need not be expressed), the right to mobility is a fundamental, natural right. This right is of heightened importance in a vast and mobile country where national myths have cowboys on horses, pioneers in covered wagons, Harley-Davidson motorcycles, drag racing, and freeways. The American history was predicated upon mobility from Europe to the East Coast, and from there to the West. And a mark of adulthood is the driver's license, a mark of growing up in childhood is the ability to cross the street and later to walk to school.

A model form of punishment or rehabilitation for criminals is to deprive them of mobility in a solemn legal proceeding. Evidently, the absence of mobility is taken as signifying the deprivation of freedom. But in regard to the handicapped, the trial is dispensed with. Incarceration may be a harsh word; but it seems an accurate one for those whose mobility is restricted.

Access to transportation, the right to mobility, is vital to the whole of social life.

United States society is generally proud of its work ethic. In large measure one's social life is generated on the job. It is the job that usually provides the money to purchase the goods and services produced by the economy. Further, work is connected in obvious and subtle ways to other parts of a person's social and psychological life. It is the future prospect of a job that redeems the investment in education (no matter how liberal). But if someone cannot get out to look for a job, what is the probability of finding work? And if one cannot get to work, one cannot hold a job.

Mobility is a right. How to assure it? Take one kind of handicapped people, those in wheelchairs. People in wheelchairs generally cannot get into buses, trains or subways. Although many probably will have no trouble driving cars, some will need vans into which their electric wheelchairs can drive, costing considerably more than an ordinary car initially, and more to maintain and insure. One solution would be to provide subsidies for private vans for those who can use them; another, to redesign buses, subways, and systems of mass transportation; still another is making wheelchair-accessible demand-response systems.

But there are many trade-offs here. Demand-response systems are segregative, as is the preferred means of transportation in this country, a private vehicle. In addition, there is a social stigma felt by people in wheelchairs about demand-response solutions to the problem of mobility. Access to public transportation is a measure that would impress the existence and capability of people in wheelchairs on an able-bodied society—perhaps that is why people in wheelchairs feel so strongly about it.

Issues of transportation are connected to other issues of public policy. It is not as if the current system of transportation in the United States grew up in a policy vacuum. Transportation is connected to society. An analysis of competing transportation alternatives can and should take account of the general needs of disabled people, including that of universally accessible mass transportation, even if in the end economic scarcity forces modification. This is especially timely with an energy shortage that has compelled able-bodied society to some inkling of the absence of mobility, opportunity, and freedom long known by transportation-disabled people.

Work

The problems of disability and the economy are perplexing. As a consumer the disabled person faces numerous obstacles in "maximizing utility." Recollect the example of transportation: What good is the supermarket if it is too far away, if the disabled person cannot reach the shelves, or bring home the food? Choices are limited beyond what they would be for an able-bodied person.

Moreover, the disabled person as consumer may have enormous problems buying suitable goods at all. The joke about the amputee continually buying shoes for the left foot and looking for a person who needs shoes for the right foot is no joke to the amputee. And consider those disabled people, unable to tie shoes, who face the dilemma of trying to find shoes simultaneously sturdy and laceless.

The current array of goods and services offered by the American economy is programmed after the need of an average person. Disabled consumers may well find it difficult to spend their dollars wisely, even with enormous effort given to shopping for the appropriate products, for many products that would be useful to the disabled person are not even on the market. Thus the disabled may be forced to modify pre-existing able-bodied devices (like those "reachers" once in use at neighborhood grocery stores) to their own needs.

Unfortunately the economy has not yet capitalized on the huge market of disabled people. For instance, the wheelchair monopoly has only recently started producing outdoor electric wheelchairs, although there has long been a need for them. Or imagine a computer which would read books—its pace could be selected, it could re-read sections ill understood. Such a device would be of clear use to blind people and, indeed, is in production. But how many other "space age" devices of use to handicapped people are not in production? How many have not even been thought of in the first place?

Limited access to goods, present marketing targets, and the absence of research and development to meet their needs are all obstacles for handicapped people as consumers. But what the disabled person buys depends not only on the goods available but on the money he or she has to spend. Since in modern society the source of money is usually income from a job, an adequate economic policy for the handicapped must direct itself to the central issues of work and income. Disabled people are not only consumers—this part of their lives has been receiving increased attention—but, at least potentially, producers who earn income.

The role of producer is constituted in relation to a contingent social structure of jobs, employment opportunity, and productive technology and organization. And the same is true with any role in a disabled person's life: A person is transportation-disabled in relation to a given contingent structure of transportation, education-disabled in relation to a structure of schooling. Of all the social contexts, however, the most important may be work.

By and large, the North American is an economy, a culture, that prides itself on its affluence, growth, and material well being. Americans take pride in their willingness and ability to take care of children, mothers, old people, disabled people, and others who do not contribute market labor. Yet at the same time, the recipients of these resources are viewed as second-class citizens because they do not work.

Strings attached or not, society provides aid for many who do not work, the money coming increasingly from the government, which gets it from taxing those who do work. These transfer payments, as they are called, redistribute money. They are an enduring legacy of the New Deal and the War on Poverty. If an old dog cannot be taught new tricks, provide Social Security. If training a mother for a job is attractive neither to the mother nor to society, provide welfare. And if someone finds it difficult to secure employment because of physical difference, is not the easiest solution to provide money through Supplemental Security Income, Social Security Disability Insurance, and other programs?

In the vocabulary of social welfare there are the deserving and nondeserving poor, the distinction being that the latter are expected to work whereas the former are not. Surely it is a matter of social progress that the disabled are counted among the worthy poor so that lack of work does not spell starvation. To demand work from people unable to work is to demand blood from a stone, as futile as it is unjust. But here is a vexation; how do we know who is unable to work? Frequently, it is presumed as a matter of course that disabled people are biologically incapable of work, a social decision pretending to describe the biological nature of things. Disabled people may find it disconcerting for presumptions to be made about and for them without them.

Many women have decided that they have to work and that they want to work. And at least some old people have asked for reformations in the social security laws so as the permit them to work without financial hardship. Should disabled people not have an opportunity to work as well? Indeed, why would society not expect them to?

Jobs today are suited to the requirements of the able body. Career ladders follow the biography of the able-bodied person. Architecture is designed not for all people but for able-bodied people. One might have thought that, in a time when the structure of society was socially directable, other possibilities would have been considered than the sometimes inhuman predilections of technology and organization. That the division of labor which could have liberated the disabled person should have enslaved him or her by not being divided according to human needs is not only a social injustice but largely unnecessary as well. Production organized by human beings can be suited to human beings.

Do handicapped people really want to work? Do they want anything to do with the anxious, monotonous, insecure, and sometimes brutal world of work? Many handicapped people want jobs, but suspect that they have suffered discrimination, like women, blacks, and other minorities, on the labor market. The weight attached by so many of the disabled to Section 504 of the Rehabilitation Act of 1973, which prohibits discrimination against the handicapped, might indicate they want jobs.

In addition, one should consider that many friendships are made through a job. No presumption of pride or satisfaction in the job is needed to realize that many handicapped people not now working most likely would want to. The alternatives to work, particularly for the handicapped person, are likely to be painful, including institutionalization, watching television, or wandering through the day. A handicapped person may in fact need work more than an able-bodied person in order to be a social human being, for much of a handicapped person's life may be lived through the job.

Related to work is the education of the handicapped. Despite the proclamations of commencement day, many do not act as if education were an end in itself. Education is conducted in the light of the future, but the expected future of a handicapped child or adult may well be dim; they may find little illumination in their education. After all, why teach a person who will spend a lifetime watching television how to read?

If the present and future social well-being of the disabled person is predicated on work, the outlines of social policy seem clear: Provide an opportunity for work for those able to. It is unlikely that this will happen without a continued rise in the power of handicapped people, and a realization by the able-bodied that many policies pursued at present are not even in their own self interest.

The model of neoclassical market economics may be used as illustration. According to this model limited resources will be exchanged in determinable ratios at any state of equilibrium. With the introduction of "money" into the model everything has a price. As a rule the higher the price offered by the consumer, the more of the commodity will be available—this is the supply of the commodity. Similarly, the higher the price asked by the seller, the less will be desired by the consumer—this is referred to as the demand for a commodity. According to the neoclassical model the actual exchange ratios (prices) in any economy are given by solving the simultaneous equations of supply and demand.

In modern market societies most people sell their labor to acquire the money to buy other valued resources. Thus "labor" becomes formally incorporable into the model just like any other commodity. The market for labor is of central importance because it affects so much of the lives of so many people, including the disabled.

A firm has an interest in "productive" labor. Those who work have an interest in higher wages and, possibly, in easier or more "rewarding" jobs. These interests of the demand and the supply side are expressed not only on the market but leak over into the government, where they may lead to public policy such as special consideration for capital investment, tariffs, and maintaining law in the relationship between corporations.

Public policy has changed the workings of the market. But there may also be corporate monopolies (or their mirror image *monopsonies*—single buyers) and other barriers to the free competition presupposed by many models of the market. Forces on the supply side and the demand side may call for modifications from the market model. Thus there are various "frictions" in the labor market. Labor may not be perfectly substitutable. People may resist moving, learning or changing in other ways. Market signals may be inaccurately transmitted, delivered, or received.

But the model has a great deal to say about how many jobs there are, perhaps where they are, and who gets them. Its shortcomings arise precisely from the centrality of labor to human life. Thus, out of self-interest, people have decided to organize into trade unions, child labor is prohibited, unemployment insurance is paid, income taxes are collected, job safety standards are posted. The list goes on to include those nonmarket measures considered necessary in a welfare state.

Current equal opportunity laws stipulate that people will not be discriminated against except on some ranking of job-related abilities. The principle of equal opportunity is not only a rejection of discrimination but an affirmation that people should be given a chance to demonstrate their capacities on a given job. However, a blind person will be less productive without having learned how to navigate with a dog or Hoover cane and the deaf person, without having learned sign language. Special education, vocational rehabilitation, medical care, vocation education and a host of other services designed to make up for a deficit in productivity of disabled workers stand ready to help the disabled person be a more suitable worker in relation to a contingent technology and organization of production. But, though necessary, such services are insufficient for two reasons.

The first reason is a variant of that same reciprocity mentioned in the introduction and voiced by many of the handicapped people who have spoken in this book. A handicap is expressive of a contingent relationship between a different body and a given society. That relationship can be altered by changing the body or by adjusting to the conditions of the society. On the other hand the relationship can be changed by altering society. The same holds true for work as a central part of society: One can change the person or change the work. But usually the handicapped person cannot be substantially changed, although he or she may come to be taught how to dissemble adjustment to prevailing societal conditions. The other way would be to change the organization of production, a theoretical possibility even if it is thought in practice to be too expensive; indeed, it may be the less expensive alternative in the long run.

The second reason why strategies to improve the productivity of the person have proved insufficient is that productivity is in part a function of other social contexts. Just as the psychiatric treatment of a person may be ineffective without attention to the family and society of which that person is a part, improvements in human capital are difficult without attachment to other social systems. A vivid example of this is the effect of work on education. Education is, as has been noted, rarely an end in itself, but is usually geared toward the world of work. With no jobs, education suffers.

Even given the extraordinary reasons for educating and rehabilitating handicapped people, policies which aim toward the increase of human capital are only half the story. By themselves they are no more likely to work than other such policies attempted during the War on Poverty. One of the lessons of the 1960s in the United States is that policies to increase human capital, at least with the hard-to-employ, are inadequate and costly. In the case of disabled persons, however, sometimes only a minor modification of a job will allow a disabled person to work whereas all the training in the world would not. What is needed, then, along with increases in human capital is increases in the number of jobs for disabled people. This point can be put into the language of economic theory.

Supply and demand are abstractions central to economics; the realities to which they refer are central to the workings of market societies like the American. Part of this economy and market society is the market for labor. At any given time that market is calibrated by the "supply," what people have to offer as producers, and the "demand," the work that needs to be done.

There is every reason to believe that disabled people have been underemployed. Traditionally public policy directed at disabled people has been more concerned with the supply of disabled people capable of work. Vocational rehabilitation, one goal of which is to teach disabled children, like all education, increases human capital or what the person has to offer to an employer. The SSI, SSDI, and Workmen's Compensation programs work on the supply side too, although in this case to decrease the number of disabled people looking for jobs.

To be sure, there are some demand policies. Institutions or sheltered workshops create demand, if artificially and at low wages. The Blind Vending Act creates demand for a limited class of disabled people. But in both cases demand is created outside of the market and segregates disabled people from the market and from that society of which the market is a part. Indeed an analysis of the 85 odd federal policies directed toward disabled people reveals that few have integrative effect. Working on the supply side alone is not enough to insure jobs and is segregative in effect.

The best way to integrate a person into a market economy is to provide public or private jobs, laws which prohibit discrimination, and laws which provide incentives for employers to hire members of an underprivileged group. All the training in the world does no good if there are no jobs. In this context Section 504 of the Rehabilitation Act of 1973 is of central importance. It prohibits discrimination against all qualified handicapped people. In this context amendments to the tax code such as that offering a $25,000 deduction to firms for the reduction of architectural barriers are exemplary, if not very far reaching, in providing market incentive to firms to hire disabled people. If society is serious about integrating disabled people into the labor market, 504 needs vigorous enforcement and the tax code needs further modification. Particularly given the vast amount of money being spent on supply side policies, it is financially wasteful not to be serious about increasing demand. If only to redeem supply policies with their intended benefit, we ought to institute more vigorous demand-side policies.

In the literature of applied economics there has evolved a quite different definition of disability or, more accurately, a definition of a different sort of disability. The definition of this "market disability" is that a person is disabled if bodily difference makes that person less productive. It is operationalized by an answer of yes to some variant of the following three questions. Have you been unable to work at all for physical or health reasons? Have you been restricted in the kind of work you do because of physical or health reasons? Have you been restricted in the amount you work for physical or health reasons? A yes answer to at least one of these questions qualifies the person for the category of market disability.

Market disability does not coincide with our everyday concept of what disability is, nor does it coincide with any notion of disability held by the people who speak in this book. It is probable that the notion of market disability is inappropriate even for an analysis of the disbursement of transfer payments, never mind the necessary statistical analysis of disability itself.

Market disability assumes that productivity is a quality rather than a contingent relationship. It makes it impossible to reach nontautological conclusions about how many handicapped people are underemployed or unemployed, and it leaves out the possibility of change and the important policy question of how handicapped people can be employed. It begs the question of the possibility of discrimination. Market disability is a category with limited use and potential for much abuse.

Unfortunately, market disability has been used as a substitute for disability itself. It is an easy slip. To the extent that this elision has occurred, it has been unfortunate and misleading. For one thing, few of the disabled people in these pages would be market disabled for many kinds of work. Perhaps they work at jobs different from those they would work at if they were ablebodied. In fact, many people not characterized as disabled are limited in jobs by reason of training in physical skill, intellectual proclivity, or other factors arguably qualifying as physical or health reasons.

At first blush there is no visible problem in the application of the market model to disabled people. Anyone, disabled or ablebodied, is employed up until the point where productivity equals wage. If it should turn out that many or most disabled people are underemployed or unemployed, this is assumed to be a "natural" fact of social life. A prosperous society will provide for their maintenance by transfer payments on the side. But with blacks, women, and members of other groups, first anecdotally reported and later documented by sophisticated econometric studies, this simple market model has been found wanting. The reality of discrimination has been uncovered and, more recently, has even been measured in dollars. Where it exists, discrimination is analogous to friction in classical physics. Like friction it can dissipate useful energy.

In principle the establishment and measurement of discrimination is straightforward. One simply finds the financial returns that a worker gets from his or her potential productivity. Thus, were a black and white equally productive and were the black to earn $1,000 a year less than the white, one should say that the black experienced discrimination and reckon that discrimination as a $1,000 a year "tax."

Productivity in baseball can be measured by the wealth of statistics known to every fan. Thus one looks at batting averages, runs batted in, errors, etc. Then one looks at salary. A black and white with the same statistics should be earning the same. If in fact the black is earning less, that counts as strong evidence for discrimination. Indeed, some time ago it was found that blacks (then) suffered discrimination, for they had to run faster to keep in the same place. Even today it is common knowledge that blacks have a more difficult time securing utility positions on major league baseball teams.

There is a similar, if less elegant and conclusive, study in the field of disability. At the end of World War II, partly as a result of an improved medical technology, there was a problem of integrating disabled veterans into the economy. The Bureau of Applied Social Research studied workers during the war and concluded that disabled workers even surpassed their able-bodied colleagues in many of the indices chosen to measure productivity—thus, "Hire the handicapped, it's good business." But of course, the results of this study showed nothing of the kind. In a smoothly functioning market one would expect similar productivities. The study says nothing about the handicapped people who were not employed. What was shown was not that handicapped people work as well or better than able-bodied ones. Rather, since they had to be a little better to hold down the same job at the same pay, it showed that disabled workers had been discriminated against, just as had black baseball players.

Both studies used reasonably elaborate measures of productivity. But even these measures must be suspect. Is it not also of interest how a baseball player hustles, plays in the clutch, and is a team player? The market rewards outside of this game are presumably rewards accruing to the attraction of more business and bringing in added money, and are contributed to by hitting home runs, flashiness, even looks and personality.

What can we say about discrimination against disabled people? Unfortunately there is little quantitative empirical evidence. Categories which might operationalize disability have not been coupled with categories of income, much less years of education, occupation, and other social data. There is a large set of data about market disability and an impressive series of studies performed on it. But market disability and disability proper are not at all the same. Firm evidence regarding the presence of discrimination against disabled people and measurement of that discrimination must await the construction of appropriate data sets.

It is unfortunate that the social sciences have not as yet become responsive to the existence and situation of disabled people; not only for those disabled but for the market economy as well. For if discrimination should exist it is a wasteful frictional drag on the machinery of the market. Here, as in other cases of discrimination, it needs to be acknowledged to revalidate the market model and restore the market to efficiency.

At least as far as the existence of discrimination, if not its measurement, there are strong indications. Aside from the study mentioned there is the testimony of disabled people, including many voices from these pages. In addition, one can explore theories of racial discrimination and discrimination against other groups to determine whether such models are plausible for disabled people.

One such model of discrimination is discrimination by "taste." An employer may simply not wish to hire disabled people. Presumably this taste can arise from the employer who may be prejudiced or have Freudian anxieties about disabled people or may simply not like disabled people. It could arise from the proclivities of disabled people themselves or by virtue of their socialization experiences. Then there are the stereotypes that handicapped people are likely to be obnoxious, petulant and without social grace. Or the employer may believe that fellow workers will not like working with a handicapped person or that customers will be uncomfortable.

It is irrelevant whether the reasons advanced for the taste are accurate (there is much cause for doubt). The point is that for whatever reason the employer prefers to hire able-bodied people to disabled people just as I prefer strawberry ice cream and you prefer coffee. Whether or not the additional money needed to maintain discrimination of this sort is a prudent investment is another matter. For in theory such discrimination is costly and will disappear in the long run if firms are competitive because it will always be to a firm's advantage to exploit cheaper labor.

In an effort to explain why firms or employers will discriminate, theories of "statistical discrimination" have been advanced, in which discrimination is the result of some sort of average judgment about a group rather than about individual members of it. Thus, given the disgraceful education of many blacks, it would be a rational decision, if one knew nothing else about a person other than that he or she was black, to hire a white instead of a black as a librarian. Given the difference in socialization between men and women, a parent is perhaps prudent under similar situations of limited information to hire women as babysitters. Of course, such statistical discrimination is self-reinforcing. If there are no jobs as librarians or babysitters then blacks and men are less likely to train for them and surely less likely to get vital on-the-job experience.

There seems every reason to believe that the same mechanisms would operate to exclude disabled people. There are many costs involved in finding out about the capability of an individual. Given the current situation in testing, interviewing, and understanding, these costs are likely to be even higher with disabled people. Statistical decisions come easier with strangers, and handicapped people are likely to be reckoned as strangers. In short, there seems every reason to expect a theory of statistical discrimination to be equally relevant to disabled people as to others.

For example, the tools of employee selection presently used discriminate against disabled people. Suppose that a written test is required to assess job skills that do not include writing, and suppose that the fine motor coordination of a disabled person is such that he or she cannot write. With no testing modifications the disabled person, even though perhaps best suited, is not chosen for the job.

Or, consider another factor in job assignation technique. At some point applications for jobs will be interviewed. The handicapped person in such an interview will probably be at a disadvantage, for the odds are that the interviewer has not interviewed many handicapped people. Irrelevant behavior may distract the interviewer from the mission of the interview. It may tend to make the interviewer think things which are not in fact true, such as that a person is shifty because she will not look the interviewer in the eye, a person cannot make decisions because he cannot grasp a hand, or that a person is inconsiderate because he or she slouches.

It has been documented that people disabled while employed who were able to return to the same place of employment as before had better jobs than those obtaining equivalent employment elsewhere. Having been accepted as peers before their disability, having friends, knowing their bosses, those returning to the same job were thus able to avoid some difficulties of demonstrating their ability to a skeptical and perhaps prejudiced employer.

One way to eliminate such difficulties in the job interview as well as other difficulties arising from discrimination against disabled people is to change employers' attitudes. It is difficult, however, to assess the effectiveness of such strategies because the literature on attitudes says little about the subject of attitude change and almost nothing about the even more important subject of behavioral change. Still, it can reasonably be inferred that at least one effective way to change the attitudes and behavior of employers is to see to it that the disabled have job tenure with them. Statistical discrimination would be reduced and harder to justify. There is a compelling argument for policies of affirmative action and other stratagems that help right the balance set askew by statistical discrimination, misleading job interviews, and tests.

Numerous and nebulous are the theories for another sort of discrimination, the "structural." One version of one of these is that it is in the rational interest of firms to divide up the labor force rather than to have it united against the interests of the firm. Whether or not this is applicable to disabled people is anyone's guess. But there are other theories of structural discrimination more plausibly applicable to them. Perhaps the most plausible is that the category of disability itself is derived from the world of work. Every economy must decide who is to be considered eligible for work. And what could be easier than dismissing the whole class of disabled people rather than confronting each one? Perhaps firms like a homogeneous labor force fearful of physical risk.

Discrimination against disability may result from the technology of the assembly line where job descriptions are rigorously fixed and where there is enormous investment in plant and industrial organization. In such an environment, even though the conditions of work are man-made, it may be costly to modify them after the needs of disabled bodies. Admitting the possibility of such modifications can threaten hierarchy and discipline. It may be easier to cluster the disabled into a group and discriminate against them.

These forms of discrimination are familiar as they have been used against various other minority groups. But the disabled person is faced with an altogether different form as well. Imagine a job requiring the use of the hands in a factory reachable only by stairs. The productivity of a person in a wheelchair for this job is zero. Imagine the same job in a factory reachable by a wheelchair. The productivity of the person in a wheelchair can be the same as anyone's. Now suppose that the first factory could be changed into the second factory at an expense of $500 covering the cost of a ramp. The productivity of the wheelchair worker is equal to the productivity of the twin minus $500 divided by the time that the disabled person holds the job. This sort of reasoning can be extended to include braille markings on elevators, signs for deaf people, and a multitude of other physical barriers. Some handicapped people can work better at a table tilted 45°, others may need special modifications to telephones. It would hardly be reasonable to speak of such unmet needs as discrimination were it not for the fact that the construction of work tables, typewriters, and telephones is contingently engineered by society and is hardly a natural given.

The very concept of productivity then needs to be reexamined. It is not some magical quality or attribute. Rather it is a relationship of a person to a process of work that can be changed not only by changing the person but by changing the work as well. Some changes in the place of work should no doubt be made; there are few arguments against the ramp. On the other hand necessary architectural changes may be too expensive for individual firms. What needs to be explored and developed is the degree of modification that would make sense to both the individual firm and to society as a whole.

Section 504 of the Rehabilitation Act of 1973 considers all the forms of discrimination discussed here as just that: discrimination. It provides for equal opportunity, removal of architectural barriers and reasonable job modifications — but leaves questions of implementation to practical experience, which may not be enough. Much research is yet to be done.

Were one to look at policies related to the employment of disabled people, one would see a plethora of supply policies and, with few exceptions, no policies affecting the demand side. Thus, there are policies that provide special education, and more recently, with the enactment in 1975 of Public Law 94-142, the Education for All Handicapped Children Act, appropriate special education, as the language goes, in "the least restrictive environment." Education for handicapped children is complex and full of many problems, and PL94-142 is an awkward, if noble, law. Among the problems with special education is one which has affected the education of blacks, women, and other minorities. The problem is that in the United States the quality of an education and the learning experience is predicated on some anticipation of future reward of which improved employment opportunity is a substantial part. No jobs, poor schooling, or, more abstractly, a supply policy (education) does not work well in the absence of a demand policy (the provision of jobs).

To make good on an increasing investment in special education, Americans may do well to increase the payoff of special education by providing jobs. Similar arguments could be made for the various other educational programs, vocational rehabilitation, and the other programs lying on the supply side. It is hard to understand why supply policies are not balanced by demand policies. Suppose there were more seriousness about the perpetuation of the category of "handicap" than about the employment of handicapped people: the current mix of policies would then be entirely rational. Its first cut has become to provide transfer payments, its second cut to improve the supply of marketable skills, but this only halfheartedly. The third cut is to segregate the disabled in sheltered workshops, institutions, or as blind vendors. Current policy, then, fosters segregation, vindicates discrimination, and does little about employment. At least this was the case until the Rehabilitation Act of 1975, all the more important and fragile for its marked change in direction.

If the nation is serious about employing handicapped people, it should take every step to insure that 504 (and 503 and 501) are rigorously enforced. It should start to appreciate that frequently costs associated with this enforcement may well be less than the benefits to society of increased employment of handicapped people. Of course, society could go further. Public jobs could be provided, or wage subsidies, perhaps more attractive to the individual firm than regulation. The current $25,000 write-off for architectural modification could be greatly expanded, and research could be conducted and findings disseminated concerning the nature of that modification. All this is in recognition of the fact, or so it seems, that if you want to employ more handicapped people you should increase the number of jobs for them, decrease the obstructions to them, and make them more attractive to employers.

It is certain that some measure of such policies would be more cost-beneficial to society than the current serving. And it may well be that a large measure of such policy would not only be satisfying to disabled people but satisfactory to others as well. Some idea of the social good needs to be imported here. In applied economics the social good is operationalized by a social cost-benefit analysis. For example, the decision to make architectural modifications may cause the individual firm to become noncompetitive in the market. A regulation requiring modifications would extend to every firm. Indeed there already is a system of laws, regulations and tax structure which says that costs that are inequitable to individuals are incurred by society as a whole, individuals deriving a new set of costs and benefits from a social decision.

This is an important point for it may be impractical to improve employment opportunity on the level of the individual case, certainly to the detriment of the disabled person and quite possibly to the detriment of society. As public policy has been used in other areas for similar reasons there seems every reason to expect its use here.

Of course notions of government could be expanded. To some extent Americans profess to believe that governments are not instituted solely to facilitate the economy. Justice, liberty, beauty, fairness, excellence, and a wide and complex range of social and political satisfactions have been counted as legitimate aims. Clearly, handicapped persons have benefited less from any such expanded view of government than have their fellow citizens.

Discrimination is a source of friction for a smoothly working market. It reduces the efficiency of the economy. If cheap oils can be found to lubricate its frictional drag society would move that much easier and create that much less smoke. Such oils are called public policy, applicable here as in other circumstances where the market needs assistance.

Needless to say, it is not only the market that needs assistance. Disabled people need assistance as well. They need assistance of a new sort, which recognizes that they suffer discrimination and puts into place (and enforces) laws against discrimination as well as providing incentives to its opposite. Discrimination is not only inefficient, it is degrading — and not only to disabled people but to society.